UNIVERSITY OF EDINBURGH
LINGUISTIC SURVEY OF SCOTLAND MONOGRAPHS

1

An Introduction
to a Survey of Scottish Dialects

An Introduction
to a Survey of Scottish Dialects

by

Angus McIntosh

Professor of English Language and General Linguistics
University of Edinburgh

Published for the

University of Edinburgh

by

Thomas Nelson and Sons Limited

Edinburgh London Paris Melbourne Johannesburg
Toronto and New York

1961

THOMAS NELSON AND SONS LTD
Parkside Works Edinburgh 9
36 Park Street London W1
312 Flinders Street Melbourne C1

302–304 Barclays Bank Building
Commissioner and Kruis Streets
Johannesburg

THOMAS NELSON AND SONS (CANADA) LTD
91–93 Wellington Street West   Toronto 1

THOMAS NELSON AND SONS
18 East 41st Street New York 17, N.Y.

SOCIÉTÉ FRANÇAISE D'ÉDITIONS NELSON
97 rue Monge Paris 5

427.9
MX8

Printed in Great Britain by
Thomas Nelson and Sons Ltd, Edinburgh

IN MEMORY OF MY FATHER
KENNETH McINTOSH
1883–1951

PREFACE

In the past half-century, the close study of living dialects has been actively pursued in a number of countries and the investigation of their interrelationships is a subject which has come to occupy a respected place among other branches of linguistic science. There is, however, a considerable difference between recognising the importance of a subject and being in a position to launch a large-scale investigation connected with it. For various reasons, especially because of the expense involved, many important areas of western Europe have not been studied systematically from the dialectal point of view; in the British Isles, not one of the four main speech-groups— English, Irish, Scottish Gaelic and Welsh—has as yet been closely examined area by area.

As far as Scotland is concerned, there is now every hope of a change in this state of affairs. In 1949 the University of Edinburgh started definite plans for making a linguistic survey of the country and a systematic investigation of both Gaelic and Scots dialects was subsequently begun. The stages by which the present position has been reached need not be discussed, but I should like here to pay special tribute to the far-sightedness of Professor John Orr, without whose persistence and persuasiveness over a period of many years before the plans finally took shape, the project would probably never have been launched at all.

There are two reasons for regarding the inauguration of this survey with particular satisfaction. First, it coincides with preparations being made by other scholars for similar work elsewhere in these islands, so that it will form part of a larger project which, it is hoped, will ultimately investigate all the dialects still surviving, both Celtic and English. Secondly, within Scotland itself, it may be regarded as one of several encouraging signs of an intensified interest in the heritage and traditions of the country, and it has a close organic relationship with some of the other studies, such as social anthropology, lexicography and the investigation of oral folk traditions and material culture, which are now being actively pursued in the Edinburgh University School of Scottish Studies and also by various other bodies. The work of the Linguistic Survey is therefore directly and intimately tied up in more than one way with a much wider field of scholarship, a far more encouraging and healthy situation than if it stood in isolation.

It is clear that a number of years must necessarily elapse before the full results of such a large-scale investigation of dialects will be ready for publication; but useful information concerning various special problems encountered in surveying contemporary Scots and Gaelic dialects will begin to accumulate at a comparatively early stage. It is desirable that some of this information should be made public as it becomes available, and this we intend to publish in a series of monographs; these will be issued separately, some of them while the survey itself is still in progress. The ultimate presentation of the main mass of material collected in the course of the entire survey is quite another problem; it calls, at least to some extent, for larger volumes which will not form part of this series at all. Such monographs as have by then appeared will not, however, be superseded by these larger volumes;

they will remain definitive studies relating to particular topics falling within the scope of the Linguistic Survey as a whole. The urgent need for a number of such monographs, on a quite wide variety of problems, is indicated here and there in the present volume.

No attempt is made in this book to give a detailed account of all the types of linguistic and non-linguistic information which the Linguistic Survey is likely to reveal; these have only been touched upon to an extent sufficient to show how an understanding of them is necessary in the designing and carrying out of a survey. The nature of the final results is better studied in detail in works which use the evidence accumulated by linguistic surveys which have already been carried out, for example, in Albert Dauzat's excellent short account, *La Géographie linguistique*, where numerous illustrations are given which draw upon the copious dialect material already collected and published in France.

Nor is it necessary, since the appearance of Professor Sever Pop's monumental work, *La Dialectologie*, to say much about the history of dialect study. But there is still room for a consideration of some of the fundamental purposes and principles underlying such work. The aim of the present sketch is to provide a brief discussion of these. I begin by considering the relationship of dialectology to other subjects, both of a linguistic and a non-linguistic nature. This leads to a discussion of the problems and obligations which face a dialectologist as soon as he considers his own activities within this larger framework. What contributions can he make to knowledge, and what fields of study will benefit from these? In this way the scope of his investigations comes under scrutiny. What shall he collect and analyse and what shall he ignore? Only when some decision has been reached about these questions, is it possible to go on to discuss a number of the more technical problems connected with the processes of collection and analysis.

I have confined myself almost entirely to Scots as distinct from Scottish Gaelic dialects; this book is specifically an introduction to that side of the Linguistic Survey which is concerned with the study of Scots dialects, and I take entire responsibility for the views expressed in it. It is addressed to readers whose own special interests are likely to be rather diverse, and the technical problems which arise have therefore been discussed as simply as possible. But I have tried not to shirk them; nor have I thought it proper to avoid certain difficulties of a kind which may not have occurred to the general reader.

I should like to offer my special thanks to Mr. David Abercrombie for much helpful advice, particularly on the matters discussed in Chapter 4; to Mr. J. S. Woolley, who is responsible for the material incorporated in the maps at the end of the book; to Mr. Robin C. Robertson, by whom the maps were drawn; to Professor Norman Davis, who read the proofs and offered a number of valuable suggestions; and to the editorial staff of Thomas Nelson and Sons Ltd for much valuable counsel and assistance. Finally, I should like to express my gratitude to the Carnegie Trust for the generous grant which has made the publication of this book possible.

ANGUS MCINTOSH.

University of Edinburgh,
    January, 1952.

CONTENTS

xi

LIST OF PHONETIC SYMBOLS
USED IN THIS BOOK

These phonetic symbols are from the alphabet of the International Phonetic Association. They have here approximately the following values:—

aː   as *a* in Southern English *father*
     (the ː indicates that the vowel is long).

ç   as *ch* in German *ich*.

iː   as *ee* in *see* (the vowel is long).

ɔ   as *o* in Scots *loch*.

x   as *ch* in German *machen*.

d, f, h, l, n, r, s, t, w   as usual in Scots.

Chapter 1

INTRODUCTORY

i

The scientific study of dialects can be approached in different ways according to the objectives and methods of those who undertake it. Like any other scholarly pursuit, the investigation of dialects is in one sense arbitrary and artificial, because what is collected and analysed is inevitably a comparatively small selection of material: for reasons of practicability and convenience and also because of the particular objectives a scholar has in mind, a mass of related material is either ignored or taken for granted. There is nothing specially disturbing or alarming about this state of affairs, which is common to most fields of study, but the fact must be recognised and kept continually in mind.

About this mass of related material, two points should be noted. First that the student of dialects must take cognisance of a number of phenomena which seem to lie outside "dialectology" proper—for example, phenomena which would normally be regarded as coming more directly within the scope of a historian or a social anthropologist or a geographer, or even perhaps an ear-nose-and-throat specialist. For without some understanding of the wider setting in which dialects are spoken and the conditions of life which have obtained during their evolution, a linguistic approach is bound to be too mechanical and to misinterpret

1

some of the phenomena. Secondly, we must re-emphasise the fact that even within the arbitrarily chosen limits of dialectology, not everything can be investigated: the student must choose and select. The problems of this selection will be discussed in detail later; for the moment we must consider the first point—the relevance to dialectologists of phenomena lying outside their own immediate field.

In these days of specialisation, it is particularly necessary that the links between one "subject" and another should be emphasised, and that we should recognise their close interdependence. In due course, therefore, something must be said about those branches of study which are most closely linked to the work of the dialect investigator. Meanwhile, we shall find it helpful to make a distinction between subjects of a primarily linguistic character and those which lie mainly outside the linguistic field altogether; a little consideration will show that the distinction is necessarily no more than rough, but it is convenient.

I shall begin by considering in what ways the study of dialects is connected with certain other types of linguistic investigation; in the second part of this chapter I shall go on to examine some of the common principles underlying the handling of these various subjects and some of the present weaknesses in the links which should hold them together. Then, in the next chapter, we shall look further afield and consider the problems of dialect investigation as viewed in a wider non-linguistic setting. No attempt need be made at this stage to define dialectology precisely. It is enough to say that it involves the study of individual dialects and the relationship between one and another; as we shall see, many kinds of approach to this

2

sort of investigation are possible, and we shall have to consider some of the more important one by one.

Our knowledge of the Scots language, both past and present, can be and has been built up in many ways, and no valid method of adding to this should be neglected. The various techniques which we employ to acquire and increase this knowledge may be compared to a series of techniques employed conjointly by detectives to build up a complete picture of a crime, or one sufficiently complete to serve its purpose. No single technique can be regarded as adequate in itself, but when we have used them all, we have at least taken into account all the available relevant evidence and put it through a process of analysis, and our picture is then as complete as our material, our technology, and our patience will permit.

Of the very great deal of valuable work that has been done on Scots during the last century and a half, it may be said that the central core has been of a lexicographical kind. By far the most common driving force behind this, until recently, has been the desire to understand as exactly as may be the meaning of the texts written in Scots of various periods. The impetus has often been of a primarily non-linguistic kind; the interest has been in the content of these texts, and a study of the vocabulary in or relevant to them has resulted from a wish to appreciate their literary worth, or to extract from them information about customs, beliefs, occupations, techniques, historical events, and so forth.

For such purposes, problems of vocabulary, and especially those connected with the meanings of words, were rightly felt to be the most seriously in need of elucidation. Had the language been rather more different than it is from

English in features other than vocabulary, for example, in morphology or syntax,[1] then sheer necessity would have forced people to give much more attention to these than they have done. But it happens that the "difficulties" of early Scots or of modern written dialectal Scots are mostly connected with vocabulary. Solve these and the morphology and syntax will more or less take care of themselves. This does not mean that these other matters have no intrinsic interest, but scholars with the above-mentioned objectives in mind have been able to afford to treat them lightly, and they have in fact usually been so treated right down to the present.

Time and again we shall have to notice that the emphasis commonly given to some kinds of linguistic phenomena, and the neglect of others, bears no firm relationship to the inherent relative interest of these judged from as impartial a point of view as possible (that is, from a point of view which takes into account *all* the ways in which the study of them could add to the sum of human knowledge), but is dictated by the special purposes people had in mind when they set to work. The pursuit of lexicographical studies is one example of emphasis. An example of comparative neglect, at least till quite recently, is the general indifference to the study of the pronunciation of living dialects. For one of the characteristics of linguistic research, for which there are good historical reasons, has been a tendency to prefer the study of texts to the study of the spoken language; this being so, and since the information about pronunciation which can be gleaned from texts is not very precise, the exact study of phonetic and related problems has been slow in developing.

---

[1] For a fuller discussion of these matters see pp. 99 ff.

4

There can be no doubt that the study of the vocabulary of Scots is, from the so-called "impartial" point of view, of very great importance; all we need regret is that it has not been accompanied hitherto by a comparably strong interest in other linguistic phenomena, especially since this has to some degree impoverished lexicography itself. The earliest great work of word collecting was done by John Jamieson, the first edition of whose monumental dictionary came out in 1808.[1] The tradition it inaugurated is at present represented by two notable enterprises which are in active progress. The first is the *Dictionary of the Older Scottish Tongue*, which is being edited by Sir William Craigie (latterly with the assistance of Mr. A. J. Aitken) and which has now reached the middle of the letter *H*. The second is the *Scottish National Dictionary*, the editing of which was begun by the late William Grant and is being continued by Mr. David Murison; the published portions of this now cover the letters *A* to *E*. In both cases, much of the material for the rest of the alphabet has been collected; the work which remains to be done consists mainly in sifting and editing this material.

Between them, these two dictionaries aim at giving information about all words and usages which may be regarded as distinctively Scottish.[2] The first comes down to about 1700, the second uses material from about 1680 onwards. These dictionaries, especially the *Scottish National Dictionary*, also aim at providing information about the geographical distribution of words and about

---

[1] For fuller references to this and all other works subsequently mentioned, see the bibliography, pp. 118 f.

[2] It is greatly to be regretted that no work on anything like the same scale exists for Scottish Gaelic.

the particular form a word has in a given area. But the total knowledge at present available about these things is not always very full, and—for the modern period at least—it is one of the major purposes of a dialect survey to contribute further information of this kind.

We shall see later that the geographical distribution of different words, and of variant forms of the same word, and of the different meanings of one and the same word, is a matter of special interest to the dialectologist. If he draws systematically on the modern dialects, he can obtain far more information of this kind than a lexicographer would consider it necessary or indeed desirable to incorporate even in a very large-scale dictionary. In this way, therefore, any work carried out by the dialectologist will form a valuable supplement to that of the lexicographer. The possible uses of this supplementary information will be discussed later.

One subject which merits special mention here is a particular branch of lexicography, the study of place-names.[1] The most casual inspection of the available material reveals its great importance. Different parts of the country (quite apart from any physical-geographical reasons) are found to have different types of names. Unlike ordinary words, the names of places tend to remain associated with particular places; they are less "mobile" than other words. Their distribution is therefore of the highest interest, for the kinds of words used in a certain area are often an indication of the kinds of linguistic

---

[1] We may note in passing that it would also be well worth while making a study of the distribution in Scotland (at all periods for which evidence is available) of personal names, especially surnames. See W. Mackay Mackenzie, *The Scottish Burghs*, p. 37.

influence that have been at work in that area. The place-
names of the Hebrides are an example: the varying
proportion of Norse names to Gaelic names in the different
islands is a rough index of the general linguistic influence
which Norse, before it became extinct, exerted on Gaelic
in these places.[1] Similarly, the British place-names in the
south of Scotland are found to vary greatly in frequency
from one area to another, and their distribution is therefore
well worth investigating.

Much work has already been done on place-name study
in Scotland, but the majority of the works published do
not satisfy the needs of modern scholarship. The
systematic investigation of Scottish place-names is attended
with difficulties which might well daunt the boldest scholar.
At any time he may be called upon to show a knowledge
of Old English, of Old Norse, of Early Welsh, of Old
Irish and of the descendants of these languages, to say
nothing of Latin and French. Moreover, the earliest
documentary evidence for Scottish place-names begins
comparatively late, and the absence of early forms often
makes the task of interpretation extremely hazardous,
a fact overlooked by some writers on the subject.
Many of the documents in which they are preserved remain
unpublished. In addition to this, a really thorough
investigation of place-names would require the collection
of as much evidence as possible from contemporary oral
sources, since many names have never been recorded in
writing at all. It is perhaps needless to add that a
systematic study of the place-names of Scotland would
be of the highest interest both to linguists and to historians.
From the linguistic point of view they are very important,

---

[1] Cp. p. 22.

because they often preserve in a semi-fossilised form material which would give us information about the distribution of dialects in earlier times.

The kind of lexicographical approach which is perhaps nearest to that of the dialectologist is the compilation of local glossaries, where the writer has deliberately set out to collect only those words he has found in use in a particular area, perhaps a village, perhaps a valley or a county. Not all the existing glossaries of this kind have been published and many areas have not been covered at all in this way. Those glossaries which have been compiled vary greatly in thoroughness and competence. Some form merely a chapter or an appendix to the history of a district or county. Some give no clear indication of the pronunciation of words nor of the range of their meanings. One of the first works of importance of this kind was W. Gregor's *Dialect of Banffshire* (1866), which is a glossary prefaced by a short discussion of the grammar of the dialect. Perhaps the two best works of this sort relating to dialects in Scotland are George Watson's *Roxburghshire Word-book* and H. C. Dieckhoff's *Pronouncing Dictionary of Scottish Gaelic based on the Glengarry Dialect*.[1]

The value of such compilations is evident, in that they give a fairly full account of the vocabulary used in one area at a particular time.[2] They may be compared to

---

[1] Dr. H. Marwick's book *The Orkney Norn* is rather different as it deals only with the Norse element in the dialect. The same is true of J. Jakobsen's *Etymological Dictionary of the Norn Language in Shetland*. (Norn is the name of the Norse dialect formerly spoken in Shetland, Orkney and part of Caithness).

[2] Watson's *Word-book* includes also words now obsolete or obsolescent, but these two types both have special distinguishing marks.

8

works which set out to give a systematic account of the flora or the birds or the moths found in one single place. They naturally lack certain of the advantages of such comprehensive books as Warrack's *Scots Dialect Dictionary* or Dwelly's *Illustrated Gaelic Dictionary*, but their strength lies in the precise information they give about the vocabulary of one area. If we possessed a whole series of works like Watson's *Word-book*, all written on similar lines (so that particular items of information in them could be compared without great difficulty, dialect by dialect), then our information about the geographical distribution of the forms and meanings of words would be very much fuller than it is at present.

For this and other reasons, the compilation of local glossaries should be encouraged; the best of these ought to be published, and copies of all such glossaries, whether published or not, should be gathered together in one place where they could be consulted by anyone seriously interested in the data they would provide. Even at so late a date as this, a Scottish Dialect Society should be founded to devote itself to this task systematically, area by area. Collectors should note that they ought not to confine themselves to the recording of rare and almost forgotten words; their completed word-list should also be rich in information about the common everyday words as well, even if many of these turn out to be identical with or very similar to words in normal standard usage. Such a word-list, though this would not be its purpose, should enable a stranger, if he so desired, to express himself in the dialect concerned, assuming only that he had a previous knowledge of its syntax.

It is evident that a series of such glossaries would have

a value of a different kind from that of the *Dictionary of the Older Scottish Tongue* or of the *Scottish National Dictionary*, and that the purpose behind them would not conflict with that of these comprehensive works. Furthermore, it will be seen from what is said later about the aims and methods of a dialect survey in the narrower sense,[1] that such glossaries would not conflict with other more specialised work undertaken by a dialectologist, but would supplement his work and supply him with many pieces of information likely to open up profitable lines of investigation to him. They would in fact fill a gap which lies midway between the special field of interest of the lexicographer and that of the dialectologist, and materially add to the knowledge of both. The composition of a really scholarly glossary is no easy matter, but it is something which interested amateurs ought to be encouraged to undertake, preferably under professional guidance.

Those who have investigated the linguistic characteristics of particular areas have not confined themselves to the compilation of glossaries and the collection of place-names, and there exist several more comprehensive descriptive studies of the language of certain districts. Perhaps the greatest contribution in this kind was Sir James Murray's *Dialects of the Southern Counties of Scotland* (1873). For though there have been more detailed studies since, this book broke completely new ground and few later works show so firm a grasp of the principles involved. Studies of this type bring us to one branch of dialectology proper, and more will have to be said about them later; their

---

[1] In the wider sense, all these studies may be regarded as part of a survey of dialects.

purpose is to describe the characteristics (or rather *some* of the characteristics) of a particular dialect. Again it is evident, as with glossaries of specific localities, that with a sufficient number of such detailed descriptions, conceived on similar lines, we should be in a very good position for comparing features of any dialect with those of any other dialect. As it is, they are not sufficiently numerous for anything like a systematic comparison, area by area, to be possible.

The kind of work discussed above deals with spoken dialects which the investigator is able to study on the spot. But descriptions can be and have been made of dialects as recorded in texts from the past, for example the dialect of Barbour's *Brus*. In such cases, the material available, however copious, is always far from complete, but this does not mean that such descriptions are unprofitable. A botanical analogy to this would be the study of the plant life of some area in a bygone age, using the necessarily incomplete but nevertheless valuable surviving evidence, for example of fossilised remains or of pollen.

ii

In the branches of linguistic study discussed so far, it is obviously possible to handle the problems involved in a number of different ways, and confusion often arises from the failure to decide in advance on the proper kind of approach; this has vitiated a good deal of the work that has been done in the past. Thus compilers of local glossaries have sometimes been careless about making sure that all the items in their collection are really in local use, and the value of their work from one important point of view is then greatly reduced. Again, they, along with students of place-names, have often shown a keener interest in providing etymologies for words than in making a systematic collection of the words themselves. It is not suggested that the collection of words or names and the provision of etymologies for them are two irreconcilable activities. The trouble is simply that in many cases the latter task has been undertaken prematurely, without sufficient consideration of the difficulties of such work, and on the basis of inadequate evidence; this in itself reveals a grave lack of understanding of the basic processes of this kind of scholarship.

Again, those who have made descriptive studies of individual dialects seem often to be torn between two ambitions. One is to say as much as possible about the dialect *as it now is*; the other is to relate its features as fully as possible to features characteristic of the Scots of an earlier date, say round about 1400, or even to those found in Old English a millennium ago. In some descriptions, an attempt is made to present the whole of the material in a way designed to elucidate and emphasise this relationship, and it seems sometimes to be assumed that this is the only proper procedure. Once again, the two ambitions are not irreconcilable; but they can result in a confusion of method which prevents either objective from being satisfactorily attained. If we are to avoid this kind of confusion and understand how it has sometimes arisen, we must be careful to note that in studying problems of language two rather distinct kinds of approach are possible, the *comparative* and the *descriptive*. These we must consider in turn.

12

There are two main types of comparative approach. In the first, items in a dialect are compared with items in the "same" dialect at some earlier or later stage of its history[1]; an example would be an investigation of one or more of the differences between Middle Scots and some modern Scots dialect. Such comparisons involve chronological factors, and it is therefore convenient to refer to this kind of approach as *diachronic.* This is the historical method; whatever features we may be concentrating upon, we are then in the main concerned with their development or evolution over a period of time, just as a historian might be with the development of one or several phenomena in our civilisation, for example, the system of criminal law, or the structure of ocean-going vessels, or the dresses worn by women.

In the second type of comparative approach, the normal situation is one where items in one dialect are compared with items in a dialect in some other area; an example would be an investigation of features wherein the present-day dialects of Peebles and Dumfries differ from one another. This in the main is the procedure followed in the various branches of linguistic geography: we may refer to it as *diatopic*, that is, as an approach involving topographical, or geographical, rather than chronological factors. These two types of comparison cannot, of course, be rigidly separated in practice, but they ought not to be

---

[1] It should be observed that it is not really the "same," being in fact demonstrably different at different periods. But it can be regarded as the same in the sense that a house remains the same house even after undergoing a whole series of alterations over a period of many years.

confused. We may now proceed to say a little more about each.[1]

The diachronic approach has in fact been the predominant one in linguistic studies until recently[2]; whenever the evidence has permitted it, inflexions, words (with regard both to form and meaning), constructions, and so on, have generally been considered in relation to what they once were. Studies of this kind are branches of what is usually called historical grammar, and there are many excellent reasons for their prosecution. The comparative investigation of a language at two or more stages of its development produces most valuable results of all kinds. What is known about some feature in it at one stage will again and again provide the answer to some unsolved problem relating to another, and this works in both directions, from an earlier period to a later and the other way round. We shall also see in due course that certain comparisons of the diatopic type lean heavily on linguistic knowledge of a historical kind, and that they cannot always be made, let alone adequately interpreted, without it. Linguistic geography may well have certain profoundly important contributions of its own to make, but the value of these will prove to be very much greater

---

[1] In this book, the word *dialectology* is used to cover all branches of dialect study. For comparative studies of a diachronic kind, the terms *historical* and *diachronic* are both used. Those of a diatopic kind I frequently speak of as *distribution studies*; they are also designated rather more broadly by the terms *dialect geography* and *linguistic geography*, which I use without any distinction in meaning. Descriptive studies are referred to as such throughout.

[2] Except in such cases as grammars designed to teach students Attic Greek, for example, or modern standard French.

if they can be fitted in turn into a framework which only linguistic knowledge of the historical kind can provide.

Linguistic geography is mainly concerned with the geographical distribution of comparable linguistic items of various kinds, rather than with the function of any of them within the system of the dialect where they occur. It is comparable to an examination of the different techniques of haymaking as now practised in various parts of Scotland, or of the administrative systems or the methods of public transport found in different parts of the country. If haymaking is examined in this way, attention is focussed on the differences and similarities of technique observable between one place and another. But the *function* of haymaking within the framework of the economic life of each place is not examined more closely than the main comparative enquiry concerning the technique itself demands. So with linguistic geography; the emphasis is likewise on regional differences and similarities; and a minute examination of the exact function which the item being investigated has within the framework of the dialect of each place is not the primary concern of the linguistic geographer.

This approach is usually associated with the study of contemporary dialects, but we may note that it can sometimes be applied to past stages of a language. But before this can be carried very far, we need a considerable body of material of more or less the same date and with well marked dialectal characteristics of one kind or another. The extant remains of earlier Scots do not fulfil these conditions very satisfactorily; it is only the living dialects which offer an abundance of evidence suitable for this kind of study, and the very dearth of dialectal evidence about the different regions in the earlier periods makes it all the more important to probe the modern dialects with the techniques of linguistic geography.

Often, such regional differences in dialect as are observed by anyone making a primarily diatopic approach will naturally lead him to investigate any possible historical causes, both of a linguistic and a non-linguistic kind, which might explain these differences. In this way, the comparison of phenomena in two or more contemporary dialects will almost inevitably lead him to examine their antecedents (if evidence is available, which is not always the case) and thus to link the diatopic with the diachronic approach. Similarly, the scholar who begins by attempting to study some linguistic phenomenon primarily from the point of view of its historical development will usually find it desirable, before coming to any conclusions, to amass whatever evidence there is for this problem from as many of the modern dialects as possible. It follows, therefore, that while we must keep the two types of comparison distinct from a technical point of view, we must at the same time emphasise their close interdependence in most of the problems with which we shall be dealing.

Let us turn now to the descriptive approach. Here the main purpose is to investigate the inter-relationship of individual items within the system of one single dialect at one time.[1] The questions that a dialect description may be expected to answer are therefore of a rather

---

[1] By some, the word *synchronic* is used to describe this type of approach. But the word is sometimes used also of comparisons between one dialect (or features thereof) and one or more others spoken at the same time. For this latter procedure, the word *diatopic* has been suggested above; this reserves the word *synchronic* for the purely descriptive process, though I do not in fact use it.

different type from those hitherto discussed. Examples would be, how many sounds has the dialect, what are they, and are they all equally important functionally? By what devices are the tenses expressed and what relationship is there between the form a verb has in one tense and the form it has in another? Under what conditions is a certain intonational pattern used rather than some other intonational pattern?

In a purely descriptive study, whether he is dealing with a "dead" dialect (say that in which Barbour's *Brus* is written) or with a living dialect (say that of Fraserburgh today), the investigator will content himself with presenting what he observes in that dialect. He can pretend, if he wishes, that no Germanic tongue of any date has survived anywhere except the Scots now spoken by the inhabitants of Fraserburgh. He can then treat this as a system with no affinities (other than those of a very remote and general linguistic kind) just as students of some American Indian dialects have perforce to do in the absence of any dialects past or present which can be shown to have any relationship to them. If he does this, the material must be ordered on an "internal" basis, i.e. each phenomenon will be described only on the basis of its relationship to other phenomena in the same system.

It may be noted that this is essentially the procedure adopted in any prescriptive grammar,[1] such as Heath's *Modern French Grammar*, which might well, if its purpose were rather different, be called *A Description of the Upper*

---

[1] A prescriptive grammar is one in which the usages of some particular form of a language are presented as the correct model for a learner to follow.

Middle Class Dialect of Paris. The merits of a description of this kind, where historical and other comparisons are reduced to a minimum, will be discussed in Chapter 7. It will be shown that traditional techniques and preoccupations have tended to make even the most recent descriptive studies somewhat one-sided. As a result, many matters which have a right to be considered important have often been neglected.

From what has now been said, it will be seen that the terms "comparative" and "descriptive" are convenient abstractions which belong rather to the realm of method and technology than to the actual events or phenomena investigated. The two types of approach may be regarded as complementary, and the potential value of each in the carrying out of an investigation of some particular linguistic problem must be carefully considered in advance. What must be stressed here is that one approach or the other has sometimes been decided upon either without much preliminary thought at all, or for reasons which have very little to do with the nature of language or of the reality of which language forms an integral part.

This brings us to a rather critical point in the discussion, because it ought at this stage to be possible to see some of the problems we have inherited as a result of the heterogeneous and somewhat haphazard ways in which the study of Scots has evolved. These problems may be classed under two main headings. The first are those which arise out of an indifference to or an unawareness of the value of some kinds of linguistic evidence which though neglected are or can be made available. The second are those which arise out of deficiencies in technique, as a result of which the available evidence is not fully exploited, no matter whether the importance of this evidence happens to be recognised or not.

In this book I do not propose to discuss in detail either the first or the second kind of problem, except where these seem to have a direct bearing on the dialect survey we are undertaking. A consideration of relevant aspects of the second kind of problem must naturally follow a discussion of the nature of the linguistic evidence available, and the purposes which a scrutiny of it will serve, for our techniques must be devised accordingly. First, therefore, we must consider the value of the linguistic evidence available, and we shall begin in the next chapter by investigating what importance and interest it may have to non-linguists.

Chapter 2

DIALECT STUDY IN ITS WIDER SETTING

In what follows I shall discuss a few of the many problems of a primarily non-linguistic nature where the evidence provided by a dialect survey may be valuable. As already noted, it is difficult and undesirable to draw any very sharp boundary between linguistic and non-linguistic subjects, but it is convenient here to make a rough distinction between them. It should be remembered throughout that dialect evidence used for the purposes I am now going to discuss must always be assessed alongside of any other information available, whether this be of a linguistic kind or not. I shall confine myself for the most part to a consideration of what may be learnt from a study of the modern dialects; due attention must however be paid to their earlier stages whenever evidence is extant which makes this possible.

The stages by which the present linguistic situation in Scotland has been reached are quite complicated, for the linguistic position a thousand years ago was extremely involved. At that time, Scotland was inhabited by a number of different peoples, including Britons, Picts, Scots, Angles and Norsemen, and at least five different languages must have been in use then in one part of the country or another. It is difficult to judge how much may be learnt about this early period from a study of the modern Scots and Gaelic dialects, but since the present situation has grown out of the very different state of affairs obtaining at that time, the facts already known about this earlier period, and indeed all intervening periods, must clearly be taken into account in making a linguistic survey.

It therefore seems advisable to urge the preparation of a detailed monograph on this subject. It should set forth what is known about the movements and distribution of the various peoples and their descendants from the Dark Ages onwards; it should give special emphasis to the linguistic implications of all the facts at present known, and call attention to such obscurities as might possibly be elucidated by the evidence collected in an investigation of dialects. A work of this kind would be a most valuable guide-book for students working on a variety of different linguistic subjects, and it would help the dialectologist to conduct his researches in a way best calculated to throw light on historical problems.

For such purposes, dialect evidence must be handled with great circumspection and too much should not be expected from it. The boundaries of linguistic features distinguishing one area from another are liable to shift, so that features formerly characteristic of one area may now be found much more or much less widely. For this and other reasons connected with the perpetual modifications of various kinds that all dialects undergo, conclusions of a historical kind cannot usually be drawn with much certainty from dialect evidence alone; they can, however, be used as a check on other evidence, or to reinforce it. Besides, in certain cases, there is reason to believe that linguistic features now distinguishing one area from another have undergone little geographical shift over the last thousand years. An example is the fairly sharp boundary between Lewis and Harris Gaelic, coinciding with a formidable range of mountains. It is likely that this linguistic boundary has been more or less in its present position since medieval times. For this reason, conclusions about the nature of the two dialects and the differences between them can possibly be used for historical purposes. Among other things, for example, the differences suggest that the Norse element was rather stronger in Lewis than in Harris, though present in both places; this is also confirmed by the place-name evidence.[1]

In somewhat the same way, it would be worth while to give some attention to the exact present-day distribution of those words of Norse origin which are peculiar to the far north of Scotland. With a few exceptions,[2] these have not spread southward to any marked degree; in fact, the whole trend of dialect development has been in the opposite direction, and in the north the influence of more southerly dialects of Scots has been felt increasingly. The present southern limit of these Norse words which are peculiar to the far north of Scotland should give us some indication, therefore, of the southern limit of direct Norse influence in earlier times; at least we can say that this probably once extended as far south as places where any considerable group of such words is still in use, and, if anything, a little further south.

---

[1] Thus the element -shader from Old Norse setr, as in names like Grimshader, Hamarshader, is much more common in Lewis than in Harris. The same is true of -sta from Old Norse staðr, and of -bost(a) from bólstaðr. I am indebted for these details to my colleague Mr. Hermann Pálsson.

[2] E.g. fishing terms which have been picked up in the north by east coast fishermen and brought south.

Many other problems of this kind are still obscure. We should like to know, for example, what dialects of Scots, and therefore what kind of incomers, were influencing Shetland when Norse began to give way to Scots there. It should be possible to supply some sort of an answer to this question. Like the dialect of any other area, that of Shetland has its own peculiarities, and the part of it on which we should have to concentrate to solve this problem would be the Scots part. If we were to examine this closely, we might be able to say whether it bore marked resemblances to dialect features characteristic of some specific part of the Scottish mainland. If so, it should be possible to say something about how Scots came to impose itself in Shetland, and from which part or parts of the mainland the influence came. The evidence at present available is rather scanty, not so much because of a lack of knowledge about the Scots elements in the dialect of Shetland, but rather because of the absence of precise information about the distribution of local dialect features in Scotland as a whole. But such evidence as there is suggests that the influence was mainly direct from Mid-Scotland and not (say) from North-East Scotland or from Caithness.

In other areas of the country there is also much to learn; here are a few questions of a kind which may be partially elucidated:

(1) From what parts of Scotland did the settlers in Ulster come? Were various parts of Northern Ireland colonised by people from different parts of Scotland?

(2) Do the dialects of Southern Scotland show any

linguistic traces of the peoples who lived there when the Angles came? If so, can anything be said about the distribution of these peoples?

(3) To what extent do the southern Scots dialects show signs of any direct influence from England in comparatively recent times?

(4) What Gaelic words survive in Scots dialects in areas where Gaelic itself is extinct? How are these words distributed geographically, and what conclusions can be drawn from their distribution?

(5) What evidence is there for marked intrusions of recent date (as a result of such things as shifts in population) of one type of dialect into areas where another was formerly spoken?

These are only five questions chosen out of many, but they are of a kind which anyone undertaking a dialect survey must have in mind from the beginning. For if he is to make any contributions towards their solution, he must in each case evolve an appropriate technique, and this technique is unlikely to prove adequate unless it takes carefully into account the precise nature of the problems requiring solution. Too often it is assumed that the mere collection of a mass of data about dialects will automatically lead to there being sufficient material available to solve whatever questions are capable of solution. In fact, each question requires to some degree a separate body of information, and there is no guarantee that a dialect survey questionnaire on conventional lines will elicit enough information for any particular enquiry of this kind. The problem then becomes one of deciding in advance what are some of the questions about which it is desirable to seek enlightenment, so that the kind of material finally selected for collection will at least have the merit of being likely to be relevant to these.

A similar difficulty of deciding in advance upon the non-linguistic (or only partly linguistic) problems to be studied is perhaps even more clearly illustrated in the case of any investigation involving the study of material culture, for example, of the types of plough or churn or haystack characteristic of particular areas, or, what may also be significant, the absence in one area of some tool or utensil familiar in another. The study of such things, as distinct from the words designating them, is not strictly the business of the dialect geographer at all, but his co-operation in their investigation can be valuable. In any case, if he is disposed to take over-lightly the problems of material culture, he will soon find that he is manipulating his linguistic findings in a dangerous vacuum.

Let us consider for a moment the ways in which the approach of linguistic geography may help the student of material culture. We must begin by being wary of assuming any hard-and-fast correlation between words and things. If, in two areas, an object has two names, this does not mean that the object is necessarily of a different pattern or size, or that it has a different function, in the two areas. Conversely, if a certain name is found in two different areas, this does not mean that it will necessarily designate precisely or even roughly the same object in each place. But for a variety of reasons, the names of things and the distribution of these names are often extremely helpful to the student of material culture. For one thing, a set of name distributions may, on etymological grounds, suggest in some cases the correct solution to the problem of the provenance of the tools, utensils, and so on, for which the names stand. As always, it is necessary to emphasise the fact that linguistic evidence in such cases must be pondered together with whatever non-linguistic evidence happens to be available.

This whole field is a fascinating example of the close interconnexion of a linguistic and a non-linguistic subject. On the one hand there is the problem of the distribution and provenance of a series of material objects; on the other there is the problem of the distribution and provenance of a series of names for material objects. Neither can be studied without the other; and again it is desirable that a dialect geographer should know in advance of some of the problems in which the student of material culture feels that further linguistic evidence is likely to prove useful. For without such knowledge, it is merely a matter of chance whether the questions he asks will elicit information with this desired non-linguistic value. Worse still, it is quite likely that any purely linguistic interpretation, on his part, of such information as he does collect will have little validity: he can only interpret the distribution of names for things if he has some knowledge of the things themselves.

All this may seem very elementary, and scarcely worth mentioning, but it is a fact that some dialect geographers have a tendency to work in isolation and to invalidate their results thereby. How gravely the results are in fact invalidated will depend mainly on the purposes to which they are putting their material; for example, a phonetic analysis can sometimes afford to neglect differences of meaning which a lexical analysis cannot.[1] Something

---

[1] See below, p. 41.

further will have to be said about this when we come to deal with the more purely linguistic techniques employed in dialectology. For the moment, it is enough to say that whenever the linguist sets out to collect information about the various words for objects in common use, for example, in house or farm, he should do so in close collaboration with an ethnographer. There are certain branches of linguistic geography for which he, as a linguist, can take sole responsibility; there are others which require teamwork, and which without this are better left alone altogether.

Other problems suggest themselves in which there is a close relationship between linguistic and non-linguistic phenomena. Dialects vary not merely because of geographical separation or isolation, but because each is in a fashion a reflex of the culture pattern of the community which uses it. As a result, the handling of Scots varies in quite subtle and interesting ways between one type of community and another. This variation (or some aspects of it) is frequently apprehended intuitively by someone who moves from one place to another; it is often very difficult to describe or analyse objectively, but it should not be neglected. Communication is after all one component of a culture pattern, and the characteristics of a particular community in this respect must be considered along with those of the culture pattern as a whole.

In general, it seems that problems of this kind should be treated in special studies by social anthropologists who have had a good linguistic training, but the implications should not be forgotten by the dialectologist: let him by all means avoid such matters and concentrate on other things; but if so he must make it clear that he is consciously skirting what is at least partially a linguistic problem simply because it is not likely to be particularly rewarding to him, or because he has not the technique to cope with it.

In all these questions, it is naturally a considerable complication for the student of dialect to have to keep in mind the non-linguistic setting in which all his raw material has its existence. But, whether one likes it or not, it should never be forgotten that investigations, both of a descriptive and comparative kind, tend constantly to lead us out of linguistic territory (which is purely an abstraction anyhow) into the wider world. If they do not, it is because the material chosen for investigation has been as far as possible selected to avoid this, and because the type of analysis to which it is subsequently decided to subject it (for there are many possible kinds of analysis) is one with as few non-linguistic entanglements as possible. Both these restrictions are sometimes legitimate and desirable, but they should not be imposed without some explicit statement about their nature.

An example may be given here of a difficulty that is specially common in the study of Scots dialects, and which arises out of the social structure and inter-relationships of the communities where they are spoken; this difficulty is often avoided by dialectologists, though if it were tackled seriously, the results should be of both linguistic and sociological importance. It arises from the fact that differences of dialect are by no means entirely regional matters[1]—people in the same place do not all speak alike. This in turn arises partly because there is one form of

---

[1] Regional dialects are discussed more fully below, see pp. 37 ff.

speech, often called "Standard English," which is used, at least for certain purposes and by certain people, in almost every area of the country. We should notice, furthermore, that it is used not only in Great Britain, but in many other parts of the world, for example, the United States and Australia. In Scotland this dialect has gradually come into more and more widespread use through being taught and used as the medium for instruction in schools, read in books and newspapers, heard from the pulpit and latterly on the wireless, and so on.

Misunderstandings about the term "Standard English" are least likely to arise if it is used only with reference to such matters as choice of word and idiom, and *not* to pronunciation; we should always keep the question of "accent" firmly separate. We can therefore say that many people, throughout the English-speaking world, speak Standard English, though when they do so it is often with marked regional characteristics of pronunciation, and not with what is often called an "English accent." Standard English, or a very close approximation to it, can be heard almost anywhere in Scotland, though with very considerable variations in pronunciation. Sometimes it is spoken with what is misleadingly described as an "Oxford accent"; sometimes the pronunciation has only a faintly Scottish flavour; sometimes it is broadly and un-mistakably Scottish. Furthermore, there are some speakers who only approximate in their choice of words and idioms to Standard English, and others again who, though they may attempt to speak it, fall short even of an approximation.

Thus there may exist in any given community a complex linguistic situation, for members of the community may differ greatly, both in pronunciation and other non-phonetic matters, in the way they talk. At one end of the scale there is, in many places, the "broad" local dialect speaker who is least affected by any influence from outside; at the other there may be someone whose speech has no perceptible regional characteristics at all. In between these extremes, there may be many intermediate types of speech, and some people will have more than one at their command, each available for appropriate occasions.

All this is already felt by the social anthropologist to be of great interest and importance, and it should be similarly regarded by the dialectologist. For in a single community there may often be, so to speak, a *network* of dialects, each inevitably influencing the others. It is therefore not possible for the dialectologist to understand the structure of any one of them without knowing something about the others, any more than it is possible to understand the make-up of the "Highland English" of a Lewisman without taking into account the Gaelic dialect which he also speaks. Let it be stressed that this is a complexity which it is easier to call attention to than to cope with thoroughly. But once more it poses a genuine problem, and if one looks forward, one cannot but feel that it is in the investigation of such matters that some of the most fruitful work of linguists and social anthropologists will be done.

We must now consider to what extent the widespread familiarity with Standard English affects the work of the linguistic geographer in Scotland. It complicates his studies in some ways, but it simplifies them in others. He is able to use it almost everywhere as a medium for asking questions, which is a considerable advantage, but he finds on the other hand that its widespread use is obscuring the characteristics of the regional types of speech side by side with which it is spoken, or even that it is replacing those regional types altogether. Though, in a sense, Standard English is itself a dialect, it should be noted here that the linguistic geographer is more particularly interested in those other dialects which are peculiar to certain areas. He will find, of course, that he must take account of Standard English, since it has to some extent or other affected the regional dialects in all parts of the country; and one of his problems will be to assess the degree to which different areas have been affected in this way. To him, therefore, Standard English is not merely a convenient *lingua franca* to use in the process of eliciting information; it is the chief influence at present disrupting the status and make-up of the regional dialects, and its effects must be investigated closely area by area. We should also note that along with the increasing influence of Standard English in the sense defined, there goes an accompanying tendency for regional features of pronunciation to be eliminated. The influence of certain roughly standardised conventions of pronunciation (as encouraged in the schools, for example) must therefore also be taken into consideration.

The purpose of this chapter is by now, I hope, sufficiently clear. I have suggested that various linguistic investigations which might properly be regarded as studies in dialectology may well elucidate problems which are not themselves purely, or even mainly, linguistic. I have indicated that this often calls for collaboration, and that it very much widens both the scope and the obligations of the linguistic investigator. He must be prepared to

31

make his approach to each problem with the technique best calculated to succeed in that instance. His function is not to carry out one sweeping linguistic survey once and for all; he is permanently at the service of the historian, the ethnologist, the social anthropologist, and others; and he should be in a position to undertake any practicable study relating to the nature or geographical distribution of dialectal phenomena which may be useful for a particular purpose.

The conclusion that we may draw from all this is that there can be no question of making a complete linguistic survey of Scotland or of any other area in one operation, with one standardised technique for eliciting all the kinds of information that are needed. It is possible, of course, to overstate the difference between the material appropriate for one purpose and that appropriate for another; but as we proceed further, it will be seen that this is nevertheless a very real difference, and that it calls for more than one approach. Furthermore, we shall find that this differ-ence does not rest only on the existence of the two types of objective which for convenience (for these too are abstractions) I have labelled "linguistic" and "non-linguistic." A little consideration will show that some investigations will have to be made systematically all over the country; in others, information will be required only from one region, in which, however, intensive collecting may be necessary. In still other cases (as with any investigation of the co-existence of "layers" of dialect in one community) much of the work can be done in a small number of selected places.

It may be felt that what has now been said calls for something too ambitious, for too many different lines of enquiry. This however is not the case; here I have merely been trying to place the subject of dialect study in its wider setting, and to show how many problems there are which claim our attention. Once we are clear about this, we may well have to limit these lines of enquiry for practical reasons, and concentrate them round a primarily linguistic centre. This more restricted plan of campaign will be discussed in detail in succeeding chapters; but it has been thought necessary here to stress the intimate interconnexion of linguistic and non-linguistic phenomena, and to imply that the carrying out of a linguistic survey without proper attention to related subjects would be like pursuing the study of neurology and ignoring all other branches of medical science. Only by keeping this basic principle in mind can we hope to see our work advancing profitably over the coming years. We may now proceed to the consideration of the handling of a linguistic survey in the narrower sense with at least some perception of its limitations, and with some understanding of the subsidiary ways in which it might be developed on special lines for the attainment of a variety of specific objectives.

Chapter 3

LINGUISTIC INVESTIGATION OF DIALECTS

Students of language, like those working in most other subjects, operate with a number of principles founded on the previous observation of relevant phenomena, and they seek constantly to perfect their own basic assumptions in whatever ways new evidence makes necessary. Accordingly, they will usually expect or hope to learn something of new theoretical importance from the observation of new material. In this way it should be in the mind of any investigator that a new study, such as the intensive analysis of dialect problems in a country hitherto not very thoroughly explored from this point of view, may have this kind of use. Furthermore, in any piece of linguistic research, the investigator should always be on the look-out for new and more satisfactory techniques; in embarking on a study of dialects he will be confronted with the need for working out such techniques, both for the collection and the analysis of material. Finally, the dialectologist, like the botanist or the anthropologist, is continually seeking to add to the total available store of information, of what we like to call "hard facts." So in a linguistic survey the linguist has the task of assembling the most important information in the most satisfactory way and of analysing it to the best of his ability. To do these things he must have techniques which in turn are based on a set of fundamental presuppositions; as the work progresses the information which becomes available to him may cause him to revise both his techniques and his presuppositions.

Whenever he is at work, he should have in mind the arbitrary nature of the separation of linguistic phenomena from other phenomena; this has been made sufficiently clear already. But even so, when he is investigating problems which are related to sociology or history, he is entitled, in making his attack on them, to use his own basic assumptions and his own techniques, provided the sociologist or the historian can tell him nothing which would lead him to modify these. The question whether the underlying problem is primarily linguistic, or only secondarily so, may not in that case radically affect his approach. The important point is that he must always make consistent use of his set of fundamental presuppositions in dealing with any of the problems which he regards as proper for him to study at all. Accordingly, in whatever he finally undertakes, there is a direct profit to linguistic theory in the testing or overhauling of his presuppositions and his techniques.

In the last resort, every type of linguistic phenomenon he investigates will force him, to a lesser or greater extent, to take account of the non-linguistic context in which it is embedded, and it matters little, so far as fundamentals are concerned, whether his investigation is being made for his own satisfaction or for the benefit of (let us say) a sociologist. His presuppositions will remain the same, and any adjustment or modification of technique made in approaching a new problem will not usually be inconsistent with them. On any occasion when it is inconsistent, then the results of applying a modified technique must decide whether they justify a modification in the presuppositions themselves.

Attention has been called in Chapter 1 to the two

somewhat separate processes, in dialectology, of comparison and description. Each is a necessary complement to the other, and good parallels to these two types of approach are furnished by other branches of study; there is no question of the two being inconsistent. By description, we understand the analysis of features in a dialect from the point of view of the interconnexion with one another which they have by virtue of being component parts of one and the same system. A full description of a dialect requires as complete an account as is practicable of the characteristics of that dialect and of the way any item in it functions in the whole. This of course involves a direct study of it from a number of angles, for example, from the point of view of its phonetic system, its morphology, its vocabulary, and its syntax. Nevertheless, it is also legitimate to make what we might call "partial" descriptions, that is, accounts of the dialect from just one angle. Thus many so-called dialect studies turn out on inspection to contain no systematic treatment of anything but what their authors call the "sound system" of the dialect in question. In other cases an attempt is made to list all the words (with their various meanings) used in a dialect, but without giving much attention to other features, for example, the syntax or perhaps even the sound system. All that need be said here is that there are no cogent objections to such partial descriptions so long as it is fully understood that they *are* partial.

In what follows we shall be concerned much more with problems of comparison than with those of description, but two preliminary points might be noted. First, that the possible theoretical angles of approach to these two types of problem are very much the same. Just as one can study the phonetics or the vocabulary or the syntax of a dialect, or all of these, so one can compare features of any or all of these kinds in one dialect with those in another or a series of others. The second point is that it will be necessary from time to time to insist that the whole foundation of the technique of comparisons rests on assumptions which imply a knowledge of at any rate some aspects of the system of each individual dialect. This being the case, it is obvious that linguistic geography, which concerns itself mainly with the comparison of a selection of features in one regional dialect with their equivalents in others, cannot do this without due regard to the function of these features within the systems where they occur. It will be best to leave the subject of dialect descriptions until these two points have been further elaborated.

Before we begin to consider what is involved in the process of making comparisons, we should perhaps discuss briefly what is meant by a "regional dialect." Everyone knows in a sense what is meant, but the word can be extremely misleading. People speak, for example, of the dialect of Fife and yet, when challenged, they will concede that the people of Buckhaven do not speak in quite the same way as the people of Anstruther. Does each place, then, have a dialect of its own, or what? Is it possible, again, to draw a line on a map and say that it separates dialect *A* from dialect *B*? For example, if one contrasts the dialect of Berwickshire with that of East Lothian, can one point to a stream or a fence or a road which demarcates the two? In fact, we shall soon discover that what people mean by a dialect is something rather vague, and that they are apt to mean different things in different contexts. Sometimes, as when they speak of

37

"the dialect of Berwickshire," they are lumping together a number of communities which, though they have much in common linguistically, do not all speak exactly the same kind of Scots. At other times they will be thinking of something less heterogeneous, such as when they speak of "the dialect of Buckhaven." In the last resort every speaker has his own linguistic idiosyncrasies and thus, in a sense, his own dialect (the technical term is *idiolect*). This difficulty of terminology cannot easily be remedied, for the word "dialect" is far too convenient to be abandoned; we must simply use it and interpret it with a proper awareness of its possible ambiguity.

We should also be quite clear about another matter. One often hears it said that such and such a dialect is "pure" whereas another is "corrupted" or "contaminated." It is not difficult to see roughly what is meant by this; certain dialects, especially in remote places, have been influenced and changed far less than others by the forces of standardisation and centralisation, so that in this sense the dialect of a remote Buchan village may be said to be "purer" than that of a village just outside of Edinburgh or Glasgow.[1] But in another and very important sense, no dialect is "pure" at all. Trade, invasions, movements of population, intermarriage, the importation of new ways of doing things, the development of new crafts and

---

[1] This must not be held to imply that it is more archaic, i.e. that it is necessarily nearer to Middle Scots. Thus the use of *f*- for *wh*- in the North-East is regarded as a "pure" feature which has resisted standardising influences. But while in one sense this is perfectly true, we should note that the *wh*- sound used in most other areas (including Glasgow and Edinburgh) is much nearer to the pronunciation current in *all* Scots-speaking areas, say, six hundred years ago.

industries—these and other factors have always been at work and no place has escaped anything like all of them. As a result, the dialect of every place in the country has been undergoing constant modification ever since it first began to be used there.

Different areas will naturally prove to have been affected differently; in one, the effect of some invasion may be particularly apparent, in another the mark of certain trade relations, and so forth. In each area, the total make-up of the dialect spoken there will thus be heterogeneous in origin; some of its components will have been there from the start, some will have been borrowed quite early, some only grafted on recently. In this way, all the modern dialects, especially in their vocabulary, turn out to be compounded of the most miscellaneous stock-in-trade picked up here and there in the course of their long and far from isolated or independent histories. Indeed, a great part of their fascination is precisely that they are *not* pure, and one of the major tasks of linguistic geography is to investigate the extent and nature of the modifications that have taken place in the different areas by examining and comparing their speech habits feature by feature.

Dialects differ at least in part according to whether the various influences have affected the areas where they are spoken or not. These influences, being diverse in kind and often also in place of origin, have not all swept in the same directions or from the same centres or with the same momentum, nor have they always met with the same acceptance or resistance everywhere. Partly as a result of all this, and partly because each has developed in its own way, quite aside from any external influences, the dialects of neighbouring areas generally turn out to

39

agree or differ, point by point, in a most complicated way, and this often makes the drawing of definitive boundaries between them difficult or impossible. The shift is likely to be gradual, like that which one experiences in travelling from a flat lowland terrain to a mountainous area adjoining it. A change is observed in one detail at one point in the journey, another two become evident a few miles further on, a fourth reveals itself still later, then a fifth and a sixth and so on. But exactly where the lowlands end and the mountains begin it is usually quite impossible to say. In some cases there will indeed be more sudden and marked dialect shifts, so that immediately after crossing perhaps a river or a mountain pass or a political frontier or some old ecclesiastical boundary, a whole group of changes may be noticed. But it is commoner to find the gradual merging described above, and the linguistic geographer is wise to organise his researches on the assumption that this is so.

Part of the business of those making a linguistic survey is to investigate where this or that particular feature, noted as characteristic of one area, gives way to another. They must also see whether the boundaries between several such features coincide geographically or not, since it is likely to be of both linguistic and non-linguistic interest to establish where, if at all, there are any of these sharp dialectal splits. Another part of their task is to consider the reasons for the boundaries being where they are (here they will probably require assistance from non-linguists) and for the kind of differences which exist between the one area and the other. All this comes within the scope of linguistic geography, the basic work of which is the collection and examination of the linguistic differences[1] between one speech area and another; in other words, linguistic geography is continually making comparisons, and plotting the distribution of contrasting phenomena. This being so, it is necessary that we should be as clear as possible about what is meant by "making comparisons," and about the steps by which we decide whether a particular feature in one area may legitimately be compared with its equivalent in another or not. It will soon emerge that the types of comparison which the linguistic geographer may see fit to make are quite numerous, and that they differ considerably one from the other; this merely reflects the fact that the differences between one dialect and another can be of several different kinds. Here are three examples of types of comparison which may be expected to "catch" at least some of the more important of these differences.

TYPE 1. The investigator is aware of the widespread existence of a certain word which in English is written "stone." He knows that the exact pronunciation of this word varies from area to area, e.g. *stane, steen, styane, stone*, but he has reason to believe that all these forms are "dialectal variants" of what he would, in simple language, call "one and the same word."[2] By this he would simply mean that if, in each area, one were able to go back far enough into the past, one would ultimately reach a stage before any differentiation in pronunciation had taken place in the different areas; i.e., historically, all the above forms

---

[1] The *absence* of differences where these might have been expected is of course also highly significant.

[2] The phrase "one and the same word" must be interpreted with the same sort of reservation that we showed to be necessary in interpreting the phrase "the same dialect," see p. 13 *n*.

descend from a single form. He decides that it would be informative to collect evidence for the pronunciation of this word area by area, and plot the distribution of the various pronunciations on a map. The basis of the comparison here, and what justifies its being made at all, is the fixed point of reference represented by the assumption that all these forms are manifestations of "one and the same word": the contrasting phenomena which he will plot on his map are provided by the diversity of its phonetic forms. Here we have a typical example of the technique of comparison: the fixed point of reference on the one hand, and on the other the contrasting phenomena which, as it were, radiate from this point. Such contrasting phenomena are "equivalents" in the sense implied on page 41.

Note that in a case like this the *meaning* of the word may not be identical everywhere, though if it is not, the investigator will have to satisfy himself somehow that it once was, just as was the case with the form. If he operates with *dyke* instead of *stane*, he will soon find that his fixed point of reference must not carry with it the assumption or expectancy of an identical meaning (or set of meanings) for this word everywhere; in fact, in some places the meaning will be "a channel for draining water," in others it will be "a wall." This however does not matter so long as the investigator has convincing evidence of some kind that in *all* areas he is dealing with "one and the same word," in the sense already defined, and not, as the two very different meanings encountered in one area or another might suggest, with two quite unrelated words. This kind of comparison is one of the most important in linguistic geography; it must be carried out by an able phonetician who will collect the necessary evidence by going from place to place. The more technical problems connected with this branch of linguistic geography will be considered in Chapter 4.

TYPE 2. The investigator is aware that a certain insect, the earwig, is known all over Scotland. He has reason to believe that, taking the whole country into account, this insect is designated by a remarkable variety of different words, many of them not etymologically related to one another. Again, he decides that it would be informative to collect these names, place by place, and plot them on another map. The necessary fixed point of reference here is the insect itself: the contrasting phenomena are the different names for this insect which are found in different places. This time it is not a question of collecting a series of forms of "one and the same word" irrespective of whether these forms have identical meanings; instead, what is being collected is a series of words all with the same meaning irrespective of whether these are etymologically related or not. Instead of a relatively homogeneous set of forms such as would arise in a comparison of Type 1, we should here have a list including the following: *scodgible*, *clipshear, gowlack, horny gollach, gellick, gullacher, forkietail, tethery erse*, and so forth. It will be clear that this type of comparison is of a very different order from the first type, and in Chapter 5 we shall consider to what extent this requires a difference of technique both for the process of collection and for that of analysis.

TYPE 3. The investigator is aware of the existence of a word *stirk*, found, with slight phonetic variations, in most parts of Scotland. But he knows that its meaning varies from place to place (in some areas it means "a young bullock," in others it means "a heifer"). So he decides to

43

plot the distribution of meanings, which in this case constitute his contrasting phenomena; the fixed point of reference is the word *stirk*. This expression, "the word *stirk*," has, therefore, exactly the same logical status as "the word *stane*" did in Type 1 above; but the contrasting phenomena are this time of quite a different order. A further discussion of this kind of distribution study will be found in Chapter 5.

These examples will show that distribution studies, which always require a fixed point of reference and contrasting phenomena, can be of various kinds. It will also be evident that certain combinations of these are possible, e.g. that the variant pronunciations and the variant meanings of a word (say *stirk*) could be elicited in the course of one single enquiry; it may even emerge on analysis that there is an unsuspected correlation between the two distributions (variations in pronunciation and variations in meaning) in such a case. At the same time, the fundamental differences between the various types of comparison should be borne in mind, and it is reasonable to assume that any attempt to tackle them all by one single technique is unlikely to prove satisfactory.

Comparisons of parallel kinds can and should be made of dialect features other than those mentioned, for the examples given were by no means exhaustive. Here are some further possibilities: types of inflexion (e.g. the ways of forming the plural of certain nouns; the way certain verbs form their past tense); syntactical phenomena; the intonational and rhythmical patterns associated with particular kinds of statement, question, etc. Some of these things present greater technical difficulties than others, and are therefore not usually attempted. This is

the case with the study of the intonational patterns found
in different areas, but the fact must be stressed that such
a topic is usually left uninvestigated not because of any
inherent lack of importance, but because a technique to
deal with it adequately has not yet been devised.

In other cases, of course, a certain type of comparison
is simply judged, rightly or wrongly, not to be worth while,
i.e. to be unlikely to produce information which will be
worth to anyone the bother involved in obtaining it. In
the following chapters I shall devote particular attention
to those approaches which seem both practicable and worth
while. But we shall do well to remember that what is
not at present practicable can only be made so by experimental studies. One of the great advantages of a linguistic
survey is that it offers valuable opportunities for such
tentative investigations; only by encouraging these can the
frontiers of the subject be extended.

Let us return to the statement made above that different
types of comparison will probably require to be approached
by different techniques. It has been made clear that no
linguistic survey can be in any sense exhaustive, and the
first problem is to assemble the maximum of valuable
information in as efficient a way as possible. This involves
a careful preliminary decision about what information is
likely to be valuable and what is not; then it involves an
equally careful consideration of how the various types of
information may best be elicited. The situation is not
unlike that which confronts a deep-sea fisherman. First
he must decide what kinds of fish it will be most profitable
to catch; then he must decide whether one device (net,
hook, etc.) will cope with every fish, or whether he must
make separate preparations for catching different kinds of

fish. It is necessary to labour this point because the inherently diverse nature of the various types of linguistic information is not always recognised, and as a result it is sometimes assumed that one method will suffice to collect them all.

The usual "net" constructed for this purpose is a single "portmanteau" questionnaire containing between one thousand and two thousand questions. Some of these are designed to elicit specifically phonetic information (relating, e.g., to comparisons of Type 1 above), others are intended to add to our knowledge of the vocabulary of different dialects (especially in the way illustrated by Type 2), others of their inflexional system, and so forth. This questionnaire is put into the hands of a field worker (or field workers) and in due course the answers are obtained from a selected number of places.

In the case of a number of dialect surveys, the yield from this single approach constitutes the sole body of systematically collected material relevant to the distribution of dialectal features. As a result, especially after its publication in large and imposing volumes, this sometimes comes to be regarded as quite definitive and final, and there is no further intensive collection of material. We may note that something similar to this happened after the publication of the *English Dialect Dictionary*. Far from stimulating people to compile local dialect glossaries, the very existence of this large work seems to have given rise to a quite false impression that little of importance remained to be collected in England.

It need hardly be said here that the evidence provided by the answers to a single questionnaire are likely to raise as many new problems as they will solve old ones. A linguistic survey should therefore be regarded as a long-term enterprise which advances by a series of steps. This implies that supplementary questionnaires should succeed the first, though the information which the first supplies about *some* problems will be adequate and definitive. A supplementary questionnaire may be of two kinds, either one which goes more intensively into particular problems in a certain area which happens to be critical for these problems (the other areas we shall assume being sufficiently covered already), or one which takes up over the whole country new lines of enquiry which information gleaned from the first questionnaire suggests as profitable. The necessity for systematically following up evidence in this way will be discussed further in the next two chapters.

We must now consider whether all the material required by the linguistic geographer should be collected by the co-operative efforts of a phonetically trained field worker and a series of local dialect speakers (informants). In discussing this problem, we must bear in mind throughout the severe practical limitations imposed on the whole plan of campaign by considerations of finance. The time taken by a field worker to fill in a portmanteau questionnaire of the kind described will depend partly on its size, but it is usually reckoned that he will get what he wants from any particular informant in about a week. In five years, working alone, he should therefore be able to get information from about two hundred dialect speakers scattered at strategic points all over Scotland. He will systematically write down all the answers to his questions in phonetic script, though we should note that by no means all the information being collected is required because of any special interest in the exact way it is pronounced.

Whether such a questionnaire aims at being comprehensive and definitive or whether it is intended from the start that it should be followed up by other enquiries later, several practical difficulties about relying solely on the field-worker technique are apparent. From the standpoint of economy, it is questionable whether the heavy task of collecting a great deal of information of primarily non-phonetic importance should be imposed on the field worker unless there is no other satisfactory way of obtaining it. In some countries there is no other way, but experience has shown that this is certainly not true of the Scots-speaking districts of Scotland. It should be added that some scholars feel strongly that everything, whatever else it may be, is phonetically important, and they therefore insist that all the material collected should be written down in phonetic script by an expert. But all this miscellaneous material, even if so collected, will certainly not provide a phonetician with an entirely satisfactory body of information about matters of pronunciation.

More will be said about all this in the next chapter, but one further point might be made here. When a linguistic geographer is carrying out comparisons of Type 1, he can only get adequate regional coverage (i.e. an informative answer from every place investigated) if he is able to count on finding that the words he is specially interested in are in regular use in each place he visits. The implication of this is that in constructing a questionnaire designed to give him information about regional variations in the pronunciation of "one and the same word," he must be careful to choose test-words which have the widest possible currency. From this point of view the word *stane* will, for example, serve admirably, because—in one phonetic form or another—it is universally used; whether it has precisely the same meaning everywhere does not matter (see page 42). What is not satisfactory is a situation in which the test-word turns out to have no local phonetic equivalent in some of the places investigated: this can arise in two different ways. It may be (especially if the word stands for some material object) that the thing referred to is completely unfamiliar in certain places. Thus any enquiry for the names for small parts of fishing boats will meet with little response inland, and many farming terms will be unfamiliar in non-farming communities. Secondly, it may turn out that though the thing referred to is familiar everywhere, quite different words are used to designate it according to which part of the country one is in.

In neither case is the result satisfactory for the phonetician. In the first case, when he goes through his two hundred completed questionnaires, he will find that he has perhaps only a hundred pertinent replies; in the other hundred questionnaires he has had to write "article not used here: no word known for it."[1] In the second case, he will emerge with fuller coverage, in the sense that he will have some kind of a word for every place. But the original purpose of his enquiry will not be fulfilled, since many of his answers cannot as it turns out be compared in the way desired. For what he wanted was to get from all over the country the variant pronunciations of the sounds (or perhaps only one sound) in one particular word; what he has got instead from his two hundred informants

---

[1] It may also happen that, even though the thing itself is familiar, there is no word for it in many places (cp. p. 72), which will equally defeat his purpose.

are the variant pronunciations of the sounds found in the (say) six quite unrelated words which crop up in one part of Scotland or another. His coverage for the sound or sounds he was specially interested in is therefore even less satisfactory than in the first situation. It may be admitted of course that what he has assembled is of great lexical interest, and that what he did was therefore worth while after all, but technically it remains a singularly unsatisfactory method of procedure to set out to acquire one type of information and finish up with another.

In any case it may be doubted whether information with this special lexical interest could not have been obtained more adequately in some other way. We shall have to consider the techniques for studying word geography more fully in Chapter 5, but one or two points may be stated in advance. It is generally agreed that the investigation of word distribution is quite important. What is not so well understood is that to get a clear picture of the distribution of certain words in Scotland, an investigation confined to anything like two hundred informants is totally inadequate, and that data from something like ten times that number are often desirable.[1] For financial reasons, it is clearly impossible to employ enough field workers to carry out an enquiry on this scale,

---

[1] A denser coverage than usually aimed at of other phenomena than words is probably also desirable. Cp. the remarks of Dauzat, *La Géographie linguistique*, p. 27, on the inadequacy of coverage in the *Atlas linguistique de la France* which investigated six hundred and thirty-eight points: "La variété des faits observés est telle—surtout au point de vue du vocabulaire et de la phonétique—que beaucoup d'entre eux ont passé au travers du filet trop lâche du premier Atlas."

and we must therefore ask whether there is some alternative technique which is practicable. The method proposed, in which use is made of postal questionnaires, will be discussed in Chapter 5. We shall turn meanwhile to some of the theoretical and practical problems with which the investigator is faced in dealing with the phonetic and related aspects of dialect study.

Chapter 4

THE PHONETIC APPROACH

The study of the pronunciation of the sounds in a dialect and the comparison of the sounds in one dialect with those in another may be regarded as the main task of any phonetician working on dialectology. A discussion of the nature of this task is inevitably somewhat complicated, but it is necessary to consider the matter in some detail.

It is a commonplace that Scots dialects spoken in two different areas will, to a lesser or greater extent, "sound different," and we must now consider what this means and by what process we can analyse the phenomena involved. We shall ignore for the present the kind of dialectal differences falling into this category which might be analysed under such headings as "intonation," "rhythm," "tempo," "pitch," "voice quality," etc., and concentrate on the often more tangible differences which involve specific sounds. Taking this restricted problem as our subject, we shall examine what is meant when we say that the sounds of one Scots dialect differ from those of another. When we have attempted to classify some of the main types of difference, we shall be in a better position to decide how important some particular observed difference between two dialects actually is, and how it is to be interpreted in linguistic and non-linguistic terms.

We might begin by observing that one of the commonest (though perhaps not most frequently observed) kinds of difference between two dialects is where the one uses sounds which are not found at all in the other. Two examples may be given. In Northumberland a uvular *r*-sound (generally called "the Northumbrian burr") is in widespread use. In the Scots dialects it is not entirely unknown, but except in a few places adjacent to Northumberland it occurs only as a personal idiosyncrasy and not as a marked regional feature. In the Glasgow area and also in and around most of the larger Scottish towns, a "glottal stop" is in common use, as in the phrase *hot water bottle*, where it occurs three times in swift succession in place of the *t*-sounds.[1] In other areas it is not used at all, except by, or in imitation of, incomers from the places where its use is well-established. Numerous other examples of this kind could be given, but these two are perhaps the most familiar. We may note that differences of this kind, described in the terms that they are above, are differences which could well be investigated by someone without any knowledge of the language; a competent Chinese phonetician unacquainted with Scots could plot the areas where the glottal stop is used and where it is not. His problem can be defined in purely phonetic terms, whereas, as we shall see, the investigation of other, at first sight similar, differences involving sounds can not.

Let us describe one of these as a speaker of some Scots dialect might put it. If he comes from the Lothians and has visited the North-East, he may say when he returns, "In Buchan they pronounce the word *stane* as *steen*."[2] Now this difference is not of the same order as the other, because the speaker's surprise is not at anything queer

---

[1] Cp. the Glaswegian who said "My name's Pa'erson, with two *t*s."

[2] Cp. the Fifer who said to the Aberdonian, "Onywye, we're no the fowk that caas *fush feesh*."

about the vowel in *steen*, a sound he has in his own dialect. In a case like this, even if the vowel written *ee* is not in fact absolutely identical with a vowel he uses himself (for example, that in *tea*), this will probably escape his attention. What surprises him is that this *ee* vowel or anything like it should be used in this situation, that is, in the word which he feels should really be pronounced *stane*. Now the situations where there is such a difference of vowel between two dialects may not always be identical from an analytical point of view, but we might consider this example a little more closely before we go on to discuss others which are not quite the same.

The difference between *steen* and *stane* is not one which has always existed. In fact, like most other dialectal differences in the Scots areas, it must have arisen in comparatively recent times: if we could go back about six hundred years we should probably find few such regional contrasts in existence at that date. In details of sound, as in vocabulary and other features, the dialects have gradually diverged, though the degree of divergence has now reached and passed its peak, and centralising influences are at work obliterating contrasts which were in evidence a few generations ago. The regional differences in pronunciation between such forms as *steen* and *stane* can be described as divergences from a common prototype, and it is often convenient to classify them on this historical basis. If we do this, we can, in a rather special sense, classify the *ee* and the *a* of *steen* and *stane* as dialectal manifestations of "one and the same sound," though phonetically of course they are as distinct as if the two words in which they occur had no connexion with one another. Such a classification is implied in comparisons of Type 1 (see page 41). In making these, we work on the assumption (for which there is usually some justificatory evidence) that we are dealing with divergent forms of what we have earlier called "one and the same word," and we attempt to define the areas where each form is in regular present-day dialectal use. The more investigations we make of this type, word by word, the more information we shall have about differences in pronunciation between dialects. This will not merely be true in the simple numerical sense that more and more differences, together with their distribution, will be revealed. For various *types* of divergence will show themselves, so that we shall also learn something about the ways in which differences of this kind can come about.

At first sight, the problem might therefore seem to be nothing more than one of accumulating a body of information about a large number of words from a large number of places, but we must now consider some of the complications. I have already noted that when the phrase "differences of sound" is used to describe the kind of opposition we have just been discussing, it has a special and quite restricted sense; the fact that a dialect uses *stane* and not *steen* does not mean that a sound *ee* is not to be found in that dialect. Another example may be given. In the North-East, in the counties of Moray, Banff, Aberdeen, Kincardine and Angus, the interrogative "who" is pronounced *faa*. In most other parts of the country it begins with the sound hw[1] as in *when*, *where*, *whaur*, etc. This in itself is an interesting fact of linguistic geography, but it should not lead us to assume that the sound hw is

---

[1] For an explanation of the phonetic symbols used in this book, see p. xii above.

unknown in the North-East in other situations (for example, in the word *wheel*) or that f is unknown elsewhere in other situations (for example, in the word *faith*). "Differences of sound" of the kind we are considering aie tied to particular words or to groups of words. It is at this point that the real complexity of the whole business of such comparisons must be discussed. We can best begin by leaving the subject of comparisons for a moment and considering the function and status of sounds within the "system" of a particular dialect.

Anyone attempting to catalogue and classify the sounds used in a dialect will soon discover that these are extremely numerous; a good phonetician may well detect as many as a hundred of them. In some types of English, for example, he might find that the pronunciation of *l* in *fall* is not the same as that in *leaf*, or that the pronunciation of the initial *p* in *paper* differs from that of the second one. In most Scots dialects he would soon discover that the sound usually written *ch* can vary considerably, as it does, for example, between the two words *loch* and *dreich*. He could show this difference by writing these words as lɔx and driːç; in the first word the *ch* has a velar or "back" quality, in the second it has a palatal or "front" quality. Each of these sounds is prescribed by the phonetic context in which it occurs; after a "back" vowel (such as the *o* in *loch*) the pronunciation is x, after a "front" vowel (such as the *ei* in *dreich*) the pronunciation is ç. Differences such as these, conditioned entirely by context, that is, by neighbouring sounds, are however without significance.

Something like the same situation may be observed in handwriting. The shape of letters varies according to what follows and what precedes them. In the hand-

writing of many people the symbol *n* is not exactly the
same shape in the group *en* as in *on*; nor is that of *p* the
same in the group *op* as in *up*. This however does not
prevent anyone reading such groups from perceiving that
an *n* or a *p* is implied in both cases, despite the fact that
the two *n* symbols or the two *p* symbols are not identical
in appearance. "Contextual" variations in sounds may
similarly be classed together as one unit, despite the fact
that they are not identical in sound; x and ç, even though
they do differ phonetically, are classed as varieties of a
unit written, in ordinary spelling, as *ch*. Thus, though
any dialect contains a great number of sounds, there is
not a significant difference between all of them. The
sound *system* of a dialect is its repertory of significantly
distinct sounds, ignoring (or rather grouping into clusters)
those variants which are due merely to context. In the
same way, the orthographic system, or alphabet, is the
repertory of significantly distinct symbols, ignoring or
grouping into clusters those variants (like the different
shapes of *p* or of *n*) which are due merely to context.

We must now consider what significance this concept of
a sound system has for dialect study. Let us begin by
saying that it is quite possible, in linguistic geography, to
ignore it, and that it has indeed for the most part been so
ignored hitherto. But when this is the case, it is often very
difficult to interpret the evidence satisfactorily. Suppose
we are studying the pronunciation of the vowel in what
appears to be "one and the same word" in two different
areas (*steen* and *stane* will serve as an example). If we
do not know something about the pronunciation of other
words in each dialect we cannot even be sure that these
two words are in fact historically identical, nor can we

tell whether this particular vowel-difference is peculiar to "stone" or whether it is typical of *all* words which, like "stone," originally contained the vowel ɑː.

As we shall see, divergences between the pronunciation of the "same" word in two different dialects can take place for a variety of reasons, and the significance, both in linguistic and non-linguistic terms, of the existence of any such pair as *steen—stane*, or *faa—whae*, will depend on our having some way of assessing what type of divergence we are dealing with in any particular case that may arise. This, it is suggested, requires not merely a good knowledge of the sound system of the prototype dialect containing the single form from which we assume such pairs in one way or another descend, but also at least a working knowledge of the systems of the modern dialects with which we happen to be dealing.

Let us now examine some types of divergence. When we say that the pronunciation of "one and the same word" has diverged, we do not commit ourselves to any implications about how this came about. We begin simply by noting that a difference of pronunciation exists between one area and another in the pronunciation of the word for "who . . .?"[1] or for "stone." Whether we make explicit reference to the fact or not, we are already classifying our material on a historical basis, for we are assuming that (for example) *steen* and *stane* have diverged from a single common prototype. We may later have to abandon this assumption in some cases, but in most it will probably turn out to be correct. If we observe a large number of specific examples of such divergences, we shall soon become aware that this has resulted in various

---

[1] See Map 3, page 117.

kinds of modifications of the original system and that the
dialect of each area will have its own peculiarities in this
respect.

Even within any single dialect a number of different
types of modifications may have been made in the original
system. We may note that phonetic change in itself need
not affect the *system* as such, provided that all the examples
of any one sound are modified in the same fashion, and so
with all the examples of every sound. If all the words
originally containing the long *a* undergo a parallel modification of their vowel (shall we say from *staan, raad, laath,
twaa*, etc., to *stane, raid, laith, twae*, etc.; where *a*,[1] *ai* and
ae all represent the same present-day sound) then the system
is not necessarily disturbed. In the same way, the shapes
of the letters in an alphabet can be modified over a period
of time without the orthographic system as such being
disturbed.

There may therefore be well-marked phonetic differences
between dialects without these having any difference in
their system. The use of the "Scots" *r* in Berwickshire,
in contrast to the functionally identical "Northumbrian
burr" across the Border, would be an example of a marked
phonetic difference, sharply defined geographically, but
implying no difference in the systems of the two speech-
areas. Often, however, what happens as we pass from
one area to another is more complex than this. For
one reason or another some of the words in a group like
the above will tend to "go off at tangents" with regard
to the development of the vowel. This kind of thing
will be noted in group after group of words, and consonants

---

[1] Strictly speaking, *a . . . e*, for in *stane* and similar cases the mute
e shows that the *a* has this value.

as well as vowels may be found to undergo unexpected modifications; the original pattern of things is thus destroyed.

This can happen in several ways, but only a few need be mentioned here. In some cases an outside influence may affect certain words in the group but not others. In one area, for example, English influence may turn out to have led to the general use of the form *wrote* instead of *wrate* without however having led to the use of the forms *stone, road,* etc. In other cases the pattern is disturbed by changes of a more internal nature. For example, in some Scots dialects, the pronunciation of the word for "two" has not changed in a fashion parallel to the other words noted above. In the Middle Scots period, the presence of the preceding **w** seems in these dialects to have prevented the vowel in the word **twaː** from being modified in the way it was in **staːn**; as a result, the vowel sounds in these two words are now quite different. At first the difference must have been very slight, and the vowel sounds in the words for "two" and "stone" must at that stage have been non-significant variants.

After a time, however, the sounds grew further apart, and in the dialects where *w* exercised this special influence, the vowel sound in the word for "two" became identical at some stage with one of a different origin, that in *blaw* and *craw* for example. At this point, the vowels in the words for "two" and "stone" had passed beyond the stage of being non-significant variants. We may say, if we like, that the vowel in *twaw* has "gone off at a tangent" as the result of a special environmental factor, whereas in *twae*, where this factor has for some reason exerted no disturbing influence, it has stayed with the main group. This is

60

true even though it happens that the special development which produces *twaw* in some dialects involves little phonetic change, whereas the development which produces *twae* elsewhere involves a considerable change of sound. In any case, in the area in which *twaw* and *stane* are now found, the elements in the sound system are no longer distributed as they once were among the words used in that area.

Other types of modification may take place. One sound may be assimilated to another originally distinct from it, because of the influence of another language. Thus in Shetland the sound *th* in words like *this*, *that*, has been replaced by the *d* sound, because the *th* sound was not known in Norn and *d* was felt to be the nearest equivalent, so that the words become *dis* and *dat*. In other cases the influence of another language may endow a dialect with an extra sound.[1] These reductions and increases in the total number of sounds in a dialect may also take place without any apparent influence from another language, but the circumstances in which this may happen are too complex to consider here.

It follows from all this that a detailed knowledge of the sound system of a dialect, or of the relationship between the sound systems of several dialects, cannot be built up from an examination of a few sample words for each sound in the prototype: a whole series would be necessary to be sure of catching all the possible lines of deviation. How then does this affect comparisons between dialects?

---

[1] Such influences as that of Norn on the Scots spoken in Shetland or that of Gaelic on the dialect of Easter Ross make it evident that to understand the details of such changes we must at certain points carry out investigations beyond Scots altogether.

The case of *twaw* and *twae* is an instructive example; *twaw* (or similar forms) is found in South-West Scotland, for example, in parts of Ayrshire, Lanarkshire, Kirkcudbright and Wigtown, while *twae* is characteristic of most of the areas to the east.[1] A questionnaire revealing this distribution, by virtue of having elicited the dialectal equivalents of "two," would not necessarily reveal that this distribution is in a sense exceptional, that is to say, that, far from being the full story about the eastern and western developments of the original long *a* vowel, it is only an example of one special development. Nor would it necessarily reveal whether the western development had resulted in the vowel in *twaw* having become the same as that in a series of words whose vowel was originally distinct from that in this word. In one sense all this does not matter, but this is only true if we remind ourselves continually that we must not generalise from evidence of this kind and that questionnaires even in their entirety cannot provide us with complete information about systems and relationships between systems. For this we need the fuller type of investigation that can only be provided by a series of thorough analyses of different dialects (see Chapter 7), and it may also be said that the more of these we have the better able we are at all stages of our work to cope with many of the problems of linguistic geography.

To illustrate this, we may return for a moment to the regional use of *f-* for *wh-* in the North-East. It so happens that this particular *f-* is in some places phonetically distinct from what we may call an "ordinary" *f*, being made by the passage of air between the two lips instead of between

[1] The distribution of these forms is very similar to that of *whaw* and *whae*, for which see Map 3, p. 117.

the bottom lip and the top teeth; this kind of *f* is known as "bilabial." Once this has been noticed, it becomes important to discover how the two *f*-sounds are related in the system of those dialects where this phonetic distinction between them exists. Are the two types, for example, kept rigidly apart, so that *fat*:"what" is always pronounced differently from *fat*:"stout"? Or do they interchange in a haphazard sort of way? Or does the bilabial *f* often tend to take on the form of the "ordinary" *f*? Where *f*- is used for *wh-*, does this apply to all relevant words or only to some? And still more important, are the answers to these questions the same in all the places where *f*- is used for *wh-*?

One other example may be given. In different parts of South-West Scotland there appear the following words for "earwig"—*gellick, gowlack, gaelick*. Their interpretation, within the wider framework of a great deal of other evidence about words for "earwig" in some way or other related to the above, requires that we should know, if possible, whether these forms are the appropriate local manifestations of "one and the same word," such as we should expect or even predict if we were able to observe a strictly parallel vowel-divergence in a number of other words, or whether their stressed vowels are not straightforward equivalents in this sense. If they are, we can regard the whole region as having originally used one particular form for "earwig" and we can describe each of the above forms as having the normal present-day vowel-divergence to be expected in the region where it occurs. If they are not, then we must either look for some disturbing influence—from within the dialects themselves or from outside—which will account for the differences while still allowing us to regard the forms as having a common prototype, or we must consider the possibility that they have not all one common origin. The point is that to know where we are in this problem, as in so many others of a similar kind, some knowledge of systems is required.

I have now touched upon some of the basic difficulties of the more theoretical kind which confront anyone investigating the ways in which a group of related dialects differ in their pronunciation. Though this background to the phonetic approach has necessarily required separate treatment here, we should note that the matters to be investigated in this way are not to be regarded as at all sharply distinct or cut off from other problems where phonetic considerations are less predominantly important, for example, in some of the studies in word geography discussed in the next chapter. The primary function of the phonetically trained field worker is to attack all dialect problems in which, for one reason or another, the exact study of details of pronunciation is important. There is no reason why he should not be used to investigate other matters as well, but it would be unfortunate if, as a result of this, he were side-tracked from the one type of investigation which he and he alone can carry out. If unlimited resources were available, it would doubtless be the right course to use trained field workers for the collection of every kind of dialect material: since limitations imposed by financial considerations are severe, we must later consider carefully whether other collateral methods of a less expensive kind are not possible which leave the field worker free to concentrate on the problems where his services can least easily be dispensed with.

Two other points might be noted here. First, it is

not necessary or even practicable to discover and plot all local characteristics of pronunciation, and it would seem wiser to deal with a comparatively small number thoroughly than to attempt to be comprehensive in this matter. In this respect the procedure advocated is similar to that suggested in Chapter 5 for comparisons of Type 2. In any case, we may note that questionnaires designed to be comprehensive, or said to be so, never in fact turn out to provide anything like exhaustive information, and it is probably wiser from the start to aim at something less ambitious.

The second point is of a rather different kind. Although the dialectologist's knowledge about many details which would help him to plan his work is often very imperfect, he may have information which enables him to focus his attention on specific problems which are peculiar to particular areas; this is perhaps especially true with regard to problems of pronunciation, of whatever variety these may be. Now the phonetician can construct a series of questions designed to amplify his preliminary knowledge of such a problem in one area; for another, equally important, but pertaining only to some other area, he will probably have to construct a different set of questions. It would therefore appear to be an erroneous procedure, even in the initial stages of the enterprise, to plan to collect all comparative material in one single questionnaire designed for use throughout the country. There are good reasons for incorporating certain questions, which are likely to be relevant everywhere, into such a questionnaire and then securing the answers to them from all areas. But it is clearly more economical and efficient to incorporate certain other questions into a series of regional questionnaires, each designed specially to elicit the maximum amount of information about problems peculiar to the region concerned. This, it may be noted, is merely an extension of a principle already quite generally accepted. A questionnaire designed for investigating the regional pronunciation of French will not, it is conceded, be right for Spanish: one designed for Irish will not work satisfactorily for Scottish Gaelic.

It may be objected that to advocate the careful preparation of special regional questionnaires implies insufficient open-mindedness, that they will indeed lead to the acquisition of further information about things of which we already have some knowledge, but that they will not reveal new and hitherto unsuspected phenomena. To this there are two answers. The first is that any questionnaire, however designed, reveals quite new phenomena if handled properly by a good field worker. The second is that we must not assume that the field worker moves like an automaton from community to community, noting down only that which is required to complete each copy of his questionnaire. He should of course deal faithfully with the particular problems which his questionnaire is designed to throw light on. But he is, after all, a man specially trained to listen to peculiarities of speech, and he cannot fail, in the course of his daily association with dialect speakers, to notice other phenomena of potential importance, even if he particularly wishes to ignore them. This being so, the field worker ought to be regarded as having a dual role: first to complete the pre-arranged task which he has been given, secondly to return with hints and suggestions of new problems which can serve as a basis for their systematic investigation later. We must therefore envisage the necessity not merely of regional questionnaires, but also of returning to a particular area to investigate something which in the nature of things could not have been thoroughly studied on the first occasion.

Having discussed the problem of questionnaires, we must now consider how the field worker is to set about his task of noting down what he hears. There is no reason why he should not be provided with "leads" but he must avoid preconceptions. Accordingly, though he may be on the look-out for certain points, he will often in fact not know what to expect and he must be prepared to handle a number of unforeseen discoveries. He must therefore be equipped with a knowledge of how to note down a very large number of sounds, and it is advisable that for this purpose he should use the appropriate symbols devised by the International Phonetic Association.[1] As he proceeds with his work in any one place he may begin to suspect that his notation has in fact often been over-precise and that for comparative purposes it is likely to be somewhat confusing. Each word turns out to have a slightly different pronunciation in every place he visits. The delicacy of his distinctions must in some way be adjusted to the objectives he has in mind, but it is very doubtful whether he can do this as he moves from place

---

[1] The phonetic notation of the International Phonetic Association has two main merits. First, it has been worked out by the joint efforts of a large number of experienced phoneticians, and its adequacy has been thoroughly tested by the successful use of it in recording the pronunciation of scores of different languages. Secondly, it is a system familiar to scholars all over the world, so that phonetic information set down in it is easily intelligible to dialectologists in all countries.

to place. His task is much more difficult than that of someone working steadily in one area, whose main problems are to sort out the relationship between the sounds in one single system. The travelling field worker has to do this wherever he happens to be working, but in addition, when he moves on to the next place, he has to decide whether *stane*, or *twaw*, or whatever word it may be, is pronounced differently here from the last place or whether it is not, and often he may be in doubt.

The handling of phonetic notation under these circumstances is an art which every investigator must develop in his own way; its successful use depends not only on technical skill, but on wide experience. And at the later stages when the evidence is being analysed, he himself is more likely than anybody else to be able to reduce his field transcriptions of a given word as pronounced in a series of dialects into some sort of system. For this reason it is wrong to impose on him the restriction which Gilliéron imposed on Edmont, who collected the material for the *Atlas linguistique de la France*. Edmont was denied any chance of second thoughts or revisions or synthesis, and it is highly doubtful whether the project benefited by this.

Here we must call attention to the fact that the material which a phonetician notes down from an informant is often and quite wrongly described as "raw material," as if he had in some way captured the actual sounds in their entirety. In fact what he returns with in his notebooks has, by the very act of being written down, gone through a stage of processing and is no longer "raw" at all. Just what the nature of that processing is will depend partly on the problems inherent in any attempt to express sounds by written symbols and partly on the competence and preoccupations of the phonetician himself. But in any case, if he has had any experience, he will be well aware of all this, and both he and anybody else who is working on the material at a later stage will have to decide what implications it has when any question of analysing the material arises. An impressionistic transcription is essentially an individual and private matter; it is not for the public eye. Some form of synthesis of the material is therefore necessary, and invariably to print the material exactly as it was first written down by the field worker would almost certainly be misleading. In the world of scholarship error can appear in a variety of forms, but one of the most dangerous is that which has a specious appearance of precision.

Chapter 5

WORD GEOGRAPHY

Word geography concerns itself primarily with the study of vocabulary from the comparative point of view which I have called diatopic. It attempts first to accumulate as much relevant information as possible about the geographical distribution of words and then to discover what may be deduced from this information. By "the distribution of words" is normally meant a study of Type 2 (page 43); that is to say, the investigator uses a fixed point of reference of the kind there described and on this basis seeks to collect from different places different words for "one and the same thing."[1]

When an enquiry of this type has been made, and information is available from all over the country—telling us, for example, what a three-legged milking-stool is called in several hundred different places—the evidence will show either that one word is used everywhere or that two or more are in use. When the assembled material reveals that more than one word is in use, it will usually turn out that each of these has a different geographical distribution, and it becomes the task of the linguistic

---

[1] Not necessarily a tangible or material object (perhaps it would be more accurate to say "not necessarily the *concept*" of such an object), e.g. an earwig or a three-legged milking-stool. It is equally possible, for example, to collect different words used in ordering a horse to turn to the left; here the "fixed point of reference" may be said to be an *intention*, i.e. the intention which in fact turns out to be expressed differently in different areas by such words of command as *hi, vain, yain*.

geographer to plot these distributions. His interest lies therefore not merely in discovering as many different words as he can which stand for "one and the same thing"; he must at the same time define as accurately as possible the area or areas where each is used.

In making studies in word geography, it is clearly impossible to look into the distribution of many thousands of words; a selection must be made and we must then concentrate on these. How then is this selection to be made? In the first place, it is usually desirable to achieve the fullest possible geographical coverage. However many different localities we may plan to investigate, all our efforts in this direction will be in vain unless at the same time we are careful to choose as the basis for our questions fixed points of reference which are likely everywhere to produce a linguistic reaction. In special cases it may well be important to make specifically regional investigations, where attention is confined, shall we say, to the areas where coal is mined, or peat is cut, or where mackerel are fished. But most special enquiries of this sort should be made by means of a questionnaire designed for the purpose and not by the more extravagant means of incorporating them in a "general" questionnaire intended for use everywhere. The main approach to word geography should be through fixed points of reference which are very widely and generally familiar; this is our first principle.

Incidentally, if it turns out that no answer to a particular question is forthcoming from certain places, it is desirable to know whether the object (or whatever it may be) is unknown there (so that as a result there is little or no need for a word for it), or whether, though the object is familiar enough, it simply has no name. An example of the first

71

would be the absence in central Perthshire of words for certain sea-fish; of the second, the frequently observed absence of names for many flowers in the vocabulary of people who are nevertheless well acquainted with the flowers themselves. The total absence of any word for some particular object, action or attribute in one place, as against the presence of such a word elsewhere, provides us in itself with contrasting phenomena. But it should be known in each case which of these two possible factors explains the failure to elicit a word at all in any one place, because it is not otherwise possible to interpret the answer to our questions.

To the linguist himself this point may often seem comparatively unimportant. But it is as well to remember that the whole complexity of the material connected with the geographical distribution of words has a socio-historical background to it as well as a linguistic one. In other words, differences observed between one dialect and another cannot always be explained by saying that these dialects have diverged by reason of some purely linguistic law which would have operated irrespective of the conditions of life pertaining in the several areas and of influences from other areas. On the contrary, the contrasting phenomena we obtain in such a study are very often a result of variations in the way of life and the degree to which any particular area has been influenced at different times by contacts with the outside world. A properly conducted study of regional differences in vocabulary should therefore teach us something about the nature of these variations and contacts.

A second principle governing the selection of material is this. In general, the value of distribution studies lies in the variety of contrasting phenomena elicited; in the type we are now discussing these consist of a collection of "different words." I have shown earlier (page 48) that for phonetic purposes it is often highly important to avoid running into this type of material, since it is useless for the kind of comparative investigation that the phonetician wishes to make. But in the case of word distribution, it is desirable that the investigator should set out to ask the kind of question which will produce the very type of contrasting phenomena that the phonetician is anxious to avoid, i.e. material of the kind exemplified on page 43. To this it may be objected that one cannot know in advance what kind of material is going to be thrown up. There are various answers to this. For one thing, a good deal of information is already available about the vocabulary of the Scots dialects, so that attention can be focussed from the start on promising leads based on existing knowledge.[1] For another, it is possible with very little trouble to increase this existing knowledge by two simple methods.

One (which has already been tried) is to issue a small number of copies (say two hundred) of short pilot questionnaires to students at Scottish universities, training colleges, etc., choosing people who will provide coverage for as many different parts of the country as possible. These questionnaires contain a number of trial questions which may or may not be strong claimants for further investigation from our present point of view; the incoming evidence usually turns out to be sufficiently informative to allow the investigator to decide which of the questions merit more intensive study and which do not. They also have

---

[1] We are much indebted to Mr. David Murison, editor of the Scottish National Dictionary, for the many valuable pieces of information he has already given us of this kind.

73

the value of giving at least some indication of which areas are "critical" for a particular problem so that, if it is necessary, particular attention can be focussed on these from the start. The other device is to institute enquiries through these and other channels, simply asking the natives of one area if they can call to mind peculiarities of vocabulary that they have noticed in another. In this way unsuspected material worthy of further investigation is liable to crop up, for speakers of both Scots and Gaelic are quite sharply aware of things of this kind, and will often act as informers in this matter with great zest.

We must now discuss another principle of selection. I have continually stressed the need for a fixed point of reference. Some words which appear at first sight to be very promising, because they seem to have a large number of dialectal equivalents in different places, turn out to be difficult to handle because they do not in fact represent a fixed point of reference at all. For example, we have attempted in pilot surveys to elicit all regional equivalents of "a good deal," "a pedlar," "slovenly," "exhausted," "to work hard." In cases like these the variety of answer has been frighteningly rather than gratifyingly large and it hardly is possible to do anything useful with such words in the kind of investigation we are discussing. Many of the variants are not strictly speaking comparable: there are fine distinctions in meaning between some of them, so that we have in fact no fixed point of reference. Despite their interest and importance, it seems better therefore not to attempt to handle words of this kind except in a special detailed investigation, and to make it a general rule to operate with things where the point of reference is less unstable.

So far we have discussed three principles on which the selection of word-geographical material should be made. There is one other which is important. A linguistic survey of any part of the English-speaking world should as far as possible be useful to those investigating other areas, and this applies to word geography perhaps more strongly than to most other branches of linguistic geography. If we assume that the application of our other principles still leaves us with a greater number of promising words than we can handle, then our selection from these ought to be made on the basis of what is most likely to be generally informative.[1] It is specially desirable that the studies in the geographical distribution of certain words in the United States should be buttressed wherever practicable by parallel information from the British Isles. The general problem of co-ordinating linguistic surveys in different parts of the English-speaking world will be touched upon in Chapter 6.

We have now four principles to go upon. The questions we ask should be about objects, actions, etc., as generally familiar as possible; they should produce responses with marked regional differences; words of vague and unstable meaning should be avoided for the most part; the questions should be parallel, as far as is consonant with the first three principles, to those asked in surveys of other parts of the English-speaking world. With these four principles in mind we may therefore prepare a list of words which we have reason to believe are suitable for this kind of

---

[1] It need scarcely be added that this selection should also be designed to elicit examples of as many different *types* of words as possible, different, i.e., with regard to meaning, to grammatical function, to source, etc.

investigation. The next step is to decide how to collect the desired information about them.

I have already stated (page 50) that a quite dense coverage is desirable. This statement is not made on theoretical grounds, but on the basis of careful observation of the correlation between quantity of evidence and the total amount of useful and relevant information to be derived from it. In the case of a number of test words, this has been investigated at various stages between our having evidence from a hundred informants and from a thousand; up to that figure there is no marked sign of a falling off in the value of each extra quota of information. In the kind of distribution problem we are dealing with, a phonetic transcription of the word used in each place is not necessary. For our contrasting feature is "complete difference of word" and not "different pronunciation of same word." Thus a phonetic transcription of the two words *branks* and *buffets* (meaning "mumps") gives us no information relevant to our purpose that is not adequately supplied when they are written down in ordinary Scots orthography.[1] It will of course be true that in the areas where, say, *buffets* is used, the pronunciation of this word will probably vary a little from place to place, and some will claim that the variations should be noted.

Except in special cases, if this is done at all, we must be clear that it is not for the sake of our main purpose, but for some other with which we are not really concerned in this type of comparison. The kind of phonetic information that would be provided by collecting all examples of

---

[1] It may be noted that the similar material published in Professor Kurath's *Word Geography of the Eastern United States* is presented in ordinary orthography.

the word *buffets* in phonetic script should be acquired in some other way, and I have already suggested that the phonetician ought to employ a special questionnaire for this. The perpetual insistence on phonetic transcription in all circumstances seems at first sight to represent a high fidelity to scientific accuracy and precision. In fact, in a case like this, it is comparable to a farmer separating sheep from cattle by weighing each of them to the nearest ounce; the "accuracy," being irrelevant to the purpose, is in fact pointless.[1]

If it is conceded that careful phonetic transcriptions are not always necessary, a voluminous body of valuable information pertinent to word geography can be assembled by a method of collection which does not for the most part call for the services of a field worker. This method of collection is made possible by the fact that there are in all Scots-speaking areas numbers of people who are keenly interested in their own local form of speech, and who are in possession of a system of orthography which will enable them to write down their own dialect words quite accurately enough for the present purpose.

It is freely admitted, of course, that the incoming material will in some cases be difficult to interpret, because the pronunciation as indicated by available Scottish orthographic devices will not always be sufficiently clear. For example, cases will not infrequently crop up where it is difficult to decide whether one is dealing with two

---

[1] The use of ordinary Scots orthography does not mean that local features of pronunciation go by any means unnoticed. On the contrary, experience shows that a quite remarkable variety of local pronunciations can be and are clearly distinguished when correspondents write down words in this way.

"different" words, or with two variants of "one and the same word." Such a situation, involving *gellick*, *gowlack* and *gaelick*, has already been discussed on page 63. Whenever there is a question of any of our different forms being nothing more than Type 1 "equivalents," or whenever for any other reason a closer scrutiny of the exact form of a word is necessary, then we can enquire more closely into the details, using strict phonetic methods; the postal questionnaire technique and the field-worker technique should be used conjointly in this way whenever necessary.

The value of a great mass of material acquired by means of a carefully organised postal questionnaire is such as to far outweigh the disadvantage that it is not written down phonetically. When a field worker visits only about two hundred informants throughout the whole country, there is a serious risk, not only that he will miss much that is important, but that what he writes down in any one place will be something peculiar to the particular informant chosen, and not in fact typical of that place at all. When, on the other hand, eight or ten times as much material is assembled by the other method, far less of importance is likely to be missed,[1] and the very quantity is a substantial

---

[1] An example may be given. Two hundred and thirty-one answers to an enquiry for the local word for *pullet* in the counties of East Lothian, Midlothian, Ayrshire and Lanarkshire have revealed thirty-three cases of the very interesting word *errack* (a borrowing from Gaelic *eireag*). The word is more common in certain other counties, but a field worker covering perhaps thirty informants in the four counties mentioned might well encounter hardly more than one or two examples altogether; he would certainly not gather enough information about the word to be able to plot with any accuracy the boundary south of which it is not used. See Map 2, p. 115.

guarantee that individual aberrations of this kind will not go unnoticed.

With these considerations in mind we prepared a questionnaire in which well over two hundred questions are asked, mainly of the kind I have been discussing in this chapter. A copy of this questionnaire has been sent to almost every rural school in Scotland and to a selection of city schools. To the areas where Gaelic is still spoken, two copies have been sent, one to be filled up with Scots dialect forms, the other with Gaelic. Each questionnaire is to be answered in the locality to which it was sent, and the teachers who receive it in the first instance are not asked to do more than see that it is placed in the hands of a suitable person, and that it is duly completed and returned in the business prepaid envelope supplied for the purpose. In general, a suitable person is held to be one who is middle-aged or older, a native of the district, and one not addicted to confusing what he has heard in local use with words he has only read in books. He must of course be able either to write down the information himself or to work with somebody who can. This questionnaire has been sent to about two thousand nine hundred Scottish schools. Other copies, numbering altogether about one thousand two hundred and sixty, have been sent to Northern Ireland, the Isle of Man, Cumberland and Northumberland, all of which areas are important for an understanding of word distribution in Scotland.[1]

---

[1] For help with the circulation of these questionnaires we are specially indebted to the following: in Scotland, to the late Mr. A. J. Belford and to Mr. G. S. Pearson of the Educational Institute of Scotland and to the Association of Directors of Education, which gave its approval and support to the project; in Northern Ireland,

The questionnaire is in book form and it is printed on a stout paper. Each page is divided into six rectangles three inches by five, two across the page and three down. The answer to any one question is to be written on the appropriate rectangle devoted to it, and use may be made of the back as well as the front if necessary. Each page of each completed book is cut up into six sections after it has been returned to us,[1] so that the information elicited about each problem is then on a separate card, three inches deep and five inches wide, which is then filed along with the corresponding card from each of the other completed questionnaires. In this way there is no need for the incoming material to be copied at all, and the danger of resultant errors, to say nothing of an enormous amount of labour, is thus avoided. The incoming answers to each question from all over the country are filed in a separate drawer and the material in each drawer is arranged county by county. Each copy of the questionnaire has its own particular serial number printed on every rectangle in it, and this is cross-referenced to another set of cards arranged alphabetically under the name of the person who supplied the information: this card also contains biographical and other information.

The questionnaire is envisaged as the first of several of

to Mr. G. B. Adams of the Belfast Naturalists' Field Club and to the Rt. Hon. H. C. Midgley, Minister of Education, who has also taken an interest in the work; in the Isle of Man, Cumberland and Northumberland, to the respective Directors of Education, Mr. H. L. Fletcher, Mr. G. S. Bessey and Mr. H. M. Spink; and to those who have helped by filling up and returning the questionnaires. The cost of producing the questionnaire was defrayed by a grant made to the University of Edinburgh by the Carnegie Trust.

[1] The books are cut up in large batches with a printer's guillotine.

this kind, though experience gained in dealing with it may lead us to design the second somewhat differently. In this first questionnaire, several subsidiary experiments have been tried. I have already alluded to a type of distribution problem (Type 3) in which variations in meaning between "one and the same word" in different areas are studied. In our first postal questionnaire some problems of this kind have been tackled; and though it is not yet possible to say how profitable this approach has been, the incoming material gives us good reason to believe that valuable information can be collected in this way. If this proves to be so, more distribution problems involving comparisons of this type will be investigated later.

Informants are also asked to identify their own pronunciation of certain words from a list of suggested possibilities or to provide some alternative form if none of those printed is appropriate. Knowledge gained in this way is not precise from a phonetic point of view, but there is already excellent evidence that this type of enquiry can provide a great deal of useful information, especially about what areas are "critical" for certain special phonetic problems. Once this is available, the phonetician can then focus his attention on these areas. There are in addition a few questions on morphology and the information so far received is encouraging; it casts considerable doubt on the widely accepted belief that this kind of problem can only be handled by a field worker.

Something must now be said about the uses of word-distribution studies of the kind we were discussing earlier in the chapter. Words as such, much more than individual sounds as such, are liable to intrude themselves into a dialect because of some influence from outside that dialect.

It is true that there are certain types of sound in some dialects which can be ascribed with fair certainty to the influence exerted upon them by another language once spoken there. But usually it is much more difficult to ascribe peculiarities of pronunciation to some specific influence than it is to do the same with words. The careful interpretation of word distribution may be expected to yield more information than any other linguistic approach about these external influences.

The material resulting from each question (e.g. "what do you call a slate pencil?" or "what do you call a porridge stick?") will usually produce a series of words, and each word will have some kind of distribution; often a particular word will be peculiar to a certain area and an adjacent area will use another word. In such a case it will be possible to draw geographical boundaries between the two.[1] When distribution maps have been prepared for every such series of words, it will be important to compare the boundaries associated with each. Are there some boundaries which are geographically identical (or nearly so) for a whole number of different words? If there are, we can define areas which differ from one another in numerous details of vocabulary, and we can then examine these areas from other points of view to see whether they are differentiated still further by other contrasting linguistic phenomena. The next stage is to attempt to relate the linguistic boundaries to other factors of a non-

---

[1] These boundaries will usually not be sharp, like a frontier line, for we may expect to find a belt of land where both words are in use. But the extreme limits of the area within which each is used can often be designated by a line on a map; the belt is then the area between these lines, cp. Map 1, p. 113.

linguistic kind. Some of the problems that may be illuminated in this way have been mentioned in Chapter 2.

After the plotting of word distributions, attention will naturally have to be given to such problems as were discussed when we enquired what is meant by "purity" of dialect. It is to be expected that certain areas, perhaps isolated one from the other and in remote corners of Scotland, will preserve in living use words which have long since disappeared elsewhere. A close examination must be made of this kind of situation, where a "newer" or an "older" word is found in a given area according to whether or not a particular wave of influence has reached and succeeded in affecting that area. For in this way something can be learnt about the nature of the main influences that have been exerted upon dialects from outside, and what tracks or leaps these have taken in the course of reaching certain places while leaving others untouched.

We should not forget here the close interconnexion between this sort of study and that of place-names. For place-names too, if systematically studied, are full of information about the nature of the various external influences that have operated at one time and another in a given area; the evidence provided by their nature and their distribution should therefore always be assessed along with the evidence provided by the nature and distribution of the other words studied by a linguistic geographer.

A further use of the study of word geography is the insight it provides into the extraordinary complexity of the make-up of the vocabulary of a dialect, a complexity, that is to say, which has nothing to do with the variety of material it may contain as the result of borrowings from a number of different languages. The oddities that crop up in any intensive investigation are of various kinds, and examples of numerous interesting linguistic phenomena are revealed in this way: the modification of form or meaning which one word undergoes as a result of being associated mentally with another; the disappearance from use of one word because of its having become formally identical with another of a different meaning; the power of metaphor, creating arresting descriptions of objects or animals which finally come to be the regular words used to designate them; the devices by which a dialect makes up for deficiencies in its system which have arisen as a result of phonetic change; the types of word (from the point of view both of form and of meaning) which are most resistant and least resistant to outside influence; the type of thing, object, etc., for which the greatest and (conversely) the least number of different words tends to be used in the different dialects; the ways in which "old" words have slowly or suddenly changed in meaning, and the linguistic and non-linguistic reasons for these; the use of slang expressions and of terms peculiar to certain trades and occupations. With the more restricted material embedded in earlier documents there is little scope for making a systematic study of many of these things; it is with the rich material of the living dialects that we can do this best. But the coverage must be extremely thorough and an approach on the lines described is calculated to provide adequate information about some aspects of subjects of this kind.

Chapter 6

SOME PRACTICAL PROBLEMS

Up to now we have ignored, or merely mentioned in passing, a number of miscellaneous problems to which some attention must now be given. Those which follow below are discussed with particular reference to distribution studies of various kinds rather than to a descriptive study made in one area, which is discussed in Chapter 7. On page 28 we called attention to the fact that differences of dialect are not entirely a matter of geography: not all speakers even in the same village or community talk the same. It happens that this state of affairs is much more prevalent in Scots dialects than in Gaelic, and we must decide how to deal with it.

It is generally possible to say that in a given community there is an "old-fashioned" type of speech, that is to say, one which, as far as our knowledge will permit us to judge, has been less affected than other types of speech spoken there, by recent influences from outside. For convenience, those who use this kind of speech can be called "resistant types": they will often, though not always, prove to have lived all or most of their lives in the area which is being investigated. They will generally be middle-aged or older, but it will turn out that some young people are also resistant types and that some older persons are not.

I have said that it is usually among people who are

already elderly that we find this "old-fashioned" type of speech best preserved in any area. To some extent this means no more than that they have preserved from their childhood usages then common which, for one reason or another, have become rarer since, so much rarer that they have not usually passed into the speech of younger people in the same community. But we should also note that people modify their speech habits much less in their maturer years than earlier, and that profound influences have been at work on the dialects since 1914. Those who grew up before the first World War have generally proved less receptive to such influences than their children or grand-children have. So they not only started in their childhood with a form of speech which was more old-fashioned, but they have on the whole moved away from it less than people a generation or so younger have from the dialect speech of *their* childhood. There are, of course, many exceptions to this general statement, for some older people change linguistically with the times and some young ones preserve remarkably closely the speech ways of their fathers.

The speech-habits of those resistant types who are already elderly will before long cease to be available for study, and it therefore seems proper, *in the first instance,* that we should give them our main attention in all areas investigated. We must not assume that they have preserved the charac-teristics of the speech of their youth entirely unchanged; they are bound to have been influenced to some extent by whatever new linguistic influences they have been exposed to, but to a lesser degree than other members of the com-munity. It is with speech as with dress: certain people are much less inclined than others to change their sartorial

86

habits; some seem scarcely to make any modifications during the whole span of their adult lives, and by examining their present habits we can learn something about the way people dressed fifty years ago and what changes there have been since. In the same way, the speech of a resistant type will serve as a kind of yardstick against which, in due course, to measure the extent and variety of linguistic innovation observable in less resistant types in any given place. Besides this, by giving due attention to it, we shall preserve precious material which is fast disappearing, and which, in the nature of things, these less resistant types could not provide.

It may be remarked that our postal questionnaire attempts to draw systematically on the knowledge of one intelligent informant in each place, but that he is not discouraged from getting additional information from other members of the community. In all cases where he knows two or more local equivalents for the subject of the question, he is asked to provide information about these; for example, which is the commoner, and whether a word is only used by certain members of the community, say children, young adults, or old people. In this way it is possible to get evidence about trends in the speech-habits of a place, to see (for example) which words are rapidly going out of use and what substitutes, if any, are taking their place.

It must be emphasised that "resistant" is a purely relative term, and that "resistance" is often a factor of environment rather than disposition, so that in some areas, for example the suburb of Morningside, it will be much less in evidence than in others, for example an out-of-the-way place like Abbey St. Bathans in the

Lammermuirs.[1] We should also recognise that any individual even of the resistant type is likely to be what is sometimes rather misleadingly called "linguistically inconsistent," i.e. he may in various ways (relating to the pronunciation of words, the choice of words, and so forth) behave differently on different occasions, and sometimes, at least, it will appear as if he were doing so in a quite haphazard manner.

In both comparative and descriptive work this may fill the investigator with alarm and despondency. But the expectation of this so-called linguistic inconsistency should be one of the basic assumptions of the dialectologist; it is a fact of language and he must be prepared to cope with it—he must regard the observation and noting down of these things as an important part of his work. In some cases, only comparative study and a historical approach will reveal which (if either or any) is the more resistant form (sound, word, inflexion, construction, and so on). However, it may be regarded as an advantage rather than otherwise when "inconsistencies" are met with, because in this way interesting phenomena are often brought to the attention of the investigator of which he might otherwise remain ignorant. More will be said about this when we come to discuss dialect descriptions.

One problem which often confronts the field worker is whether his enquiry in a particular place should be carried

---

[1] We have already discussed (p. 38) the general problem of whole *areas* which might be described as more or as less resistant than others. Here too, of course, the environmental factors which have controlled in one way or another the amount of influence to which each has been exposed over the centuries is much more important than any conscious element of resistance.

out with one speaker as the informant for every item, or with two or more, each contributing his share. It is obvious that the nature of the questionnaire he is working with must very often be a decisive factor here. Experience has shown that a conventional portmanteau questionnaire cannot be filled in completely with the help of only one person; the housewife lets one down on agricultural terms, the farmer on kitchen terms, and often some local expert has to be hunted out specially to deal with such items as flowers or birds.

I have already, however, expressed certain doubts about the wisdom of putting a questionnaire of this kind into the hands of a field worker and have suggested that in general his questionnaire should contain items which are as universally familiar as possible. One ought at least to be able to count on all but a very few items being known to any one good informant; this is necessary since it is desirable for various reasons that phonetic and related information should be obtained by the process of working steadily and systematically with one informant. If it seems advisable to make use of a second informant, then it is much more valuable to go through the *whole* of the material with him, using him as a check on the first, than to have some of the questions answered by the first informant, the remainder by the second. But the field worker will find the second procedure forced upon him unless the questionnaire satisfies the condition I have described.

The question is sometimes asked whether the field worker, in selecting informants, should follow any rules about such things as age, sex, or their possession of a good set of teeth. As to age, I have noted that we must not accept automatically the principle that age is an accurate index of "resistance" in the sense defined. As to sex, there is no evidence which shows conclusively whether men or women make better informants in Scotland. Finally, the disadvantages of toothlessness can be greatly over-rated, since some people without teeth are far better speakers than others with; besides, we should note that if in a given area it is a very common thing to be deficient in this respect, then this in itself may be of considerable phonetic significance, just as is the case with the heavy incidence of adenoidal trouble in some areas. For in such situations it is possible for phonetic characteristics originally peculiar to those suffering from some defect or ailment to be generalised by being adopted by others in the community who do not suffer from them. Provided that the field worker can be relied upon to recognise a resistant type when he meets one, none of these questions compares in importance with factors like willing co-operation, an understanding of what the field worker is getting at, and availability in terms of sheer man-hours.

This brings us to another point which is of considerable practical importance. It is felt by some investigators that the field worker should elicit the desired information by a quite rigid method of question and answer. The questions are to be asked in a particular form and the first response (unless it indicates a palpable misunderstanding of the question) is held to be the "correct" one, and it is noted down accordingly. The main argument for the fixed type of question is that it avoids putting wrong ideas into an informant's head. It seems somehow to be felt that a standardised form of question provides a perfectly neutral linguistic expression of what we have called the fixed point of reference. What does not seem to have been realised is that such a question, framed in Standard English and posed in the field worker's normal accent (whatever that may happen to be), will be by no means certain to produce in the so-called "naive informant" the expected neutral reaction or obviate the inducing of linguistically undesirable responses. Besides, this method wastes a good deal of time, for even apparently well-worded questions quite often fail to elicit the kind of answer wanted.

It is impractical to make anything like consistent use of the alternative method of simply pointing to the objects, etc., and asking for their names. There are several reasons for this; these objects (unless any reference to them has purposely been avoided in the questionnaire), may turn out to be distant or otherwise difficult to get at (e.g. certain trees, parts of a plough); they may be out of season (e.g. flowers, stooks of corn); the linguistic response to seeing an object pointed at will not necessarily be what was wanted; and finally, many items in the question-naire will not refer to articles or objects at all. No doubt the method might have its value in a restricted number of cases (e.g. common objects in certain parts of the house) and something further on these lines could well be done (though it would be somewhat expensive and not without its pitfalls) with the aid of an adequate set of pictures.

Experience suggests that in Scotland good informants will respond best to interrogation of a less cut-and-dried type. They have been used to thinking, however un-systematically, about the relationship between their own and other forms of Scots and between Scots and English, and they will not react in a linguistically unsophisticated way, no matter how they are questioned. The real problem is first to gain the interest and co-operation of the informant. This can usually be done by making it clear that what he has to offer is something unique and valuable, and by explaining as far as possible what the purpose of the enquiry is. Since no two informants are temperamentally identical, a flexible and informal procedure is necessary, in which the material can be elicited in a manner most suitable to the particular *rapport* that exists between the field worker and the informant with whom he happens to be working at any given time. It is a human problem and it must be solved accordingly.

Once it is solved, the advantages on both sides will be considerable, and the long business of interrogation will be turned into something pleasurable to both parties. Not only are good relations likely to be maintained once the informant understands the importance of his contributions, but the information elicited is likely to be far more accurate and complete when it is the result of two intelligent minds working together for one end. The more rigid method of strict questioning and answering is deceptively simple, and though it may have advantages in certain cases and for eliciting certain types of information, it cannot be regarded as a basically satisfactory method in general. We may note, incidentally, that little consideration seems to have been given to the question of whether certain *kinds* of information can be more successfully elicited by the informal approach than others.

Another problem is to decide what is the proper density of coverage to aim at with any type of questionnaire, and which places should be selected. How many and which places shall the field worker visit? To how many, and which, places shall a postal questionnaire be sent? The second question is perhaps easier to answer than the first. It is hoped that by sending a questionnaire to almost every rural school and to a selection of city schools (see page 79) the coverage will be adequate. It may of course be more than adequate for some questions, but this does not matter, and in any case preliminary information is not usually sufficiently precise about things of this kind for us to be able to say whether it will be or not. Indeed, the main difficulty in this whole problem is that an accurate answer to "how many and which places?" can scarcely, in the nature of things, be given in advance. One does not know how one should have carried out the experiment till it is well under way.

This is why it is so necessary to conceive of a linguistic survey as proceeding by a series of steps. The first experiment will show errors in technique. It may be that more places than necessary have been investigated to settle one question, and yet not enough to settle another. It may also turn out that the kind, as distinct from the amount, of information obtained proves to be tantalisingly incomplete because the questions designed to elicit it have not been quite adequate; this again is something that cannot always be provided for in advance, for it is naturally impossible to predict in detail what information will turn up, or to foresee the kind of complication that has in fact made some question inadequate. Everything therefore points to the need for following up some of the first enquiries by further special enquiries, either by means of a field worker or a postal questionnaire, depending on the nature of the problem.

A good deal has already been said about types of questionnaire and the kind of questions which each might contain.

So far, however, I have just touched on a related problem. Linguistic surveys are being or will be carried out in other parts of the English-speaking world and it is naturally desirable that (however they are executed) they should each assemble material which can be co-ordinated with the findings of the others. At first sight this may seem a simple enough business. Why not see to it, it may be asked, that the questionnaires of each survey produce their particular answers to the same general set of problems? If the matter were really so simple, this would be an extremely satisfactory form of procedure. But there is one very considerable difficulty. It is in fact a fallacy to speak at all of "the same general set of problems"; there are some questions which are highly pertinent to a survey of American English which have no relevance or sometimes even meaning in a survey of Scottish dialects, for example, enquiries such as "What word do you have for *skunk* and for *chipmunk*?" Conversely there seem to be few places in the United States where there is a dialect word for *earwig*, so that a problem which is important here is irrelevant there. Similar discrepancies arise in considering other matters, for example, those relating to the phonetic systems of the dialects of different parts of the English-speaking world, or to their inflexional systems. In the nature of things this too is inevitable.

Now it might be suggested that despite the irrelevance of certain problems to some areas, they ought still to be covered there for good measure. Theoretically there is support for this in the fact that the absence of chipmunks in Scotland does not mean that an informative linguistic link might not be revealed between the American words for the chipmunk and the Scottish words for some similar but not identical creature, e.g. the grey squirrel: if so, we should be dealing with a comparison of Type 3. For this reason, therefore, the question of what is unlikely to be relevant ought to be pondered seriously. On the other hand, it is quite evident that the survey of one area of the English-speaking world (in this case Scotland) ought not to confine itself to the collecting of information about matters which are important in other areas.

It will be clear from what has been said in earlier chapters that many of the problems which a linguistic survey might help to solve are problems specifically connected with Scotland and adjacent areas. These will not be solved by adherence to any kind of master-questionnaire designed for use throughout the whole English-speaking world. The correct solution to this whole question seems to be: first, that as generous an amount of attention as possible ought to be given in a Scottish survey to any problems likely to be of interest far beyond Scotland even if in some cases the results are negative, and second, that this should not be allowed to side-track the survey from as thorough an investigation as possible of what are felt to be more specifically local problems.

We must turn now to another matter: the analysis and presentation of results. As I noted earlier, it is often assumed that the gleanings of a questionnaire, at least those collected by a field worker, are to be considered as "raw material." I have said that no material can be considered "raw" once it has been written down and abstracted from the context it had when it was a part of living speech. What we have in fact is a body of material which, partly because it is *not* raw, requires the most careful handling and analysis. It is sometimes further

95

assumed that it is proper to publish this material just as it stands; the usual procedure has been to present it on maps, each of which shows the distribution of one set of contrasting phenomena.

I would suggest here that the peculiar nature of the assembled material raises special problems regarding its presentation. It is, to begin with, an arbitrary selection of material (no matter how good or how "scientific" the reasons for that selection) which has been collected at the cost of ignoring much else of importance. Moreover, having been written down (by no matter how experienced a field worker), it is liable to be erroneous, because of some mishearing, for example, or some slip of the pen or some misunderstanding of a question. Besides, as we have already seen (page 68), the original impressionistic transcriptions of a field worker should not represent his last word on the material he has collected. For these and other reasons, this material must to some extent be analysed and edited before publication; it is not sufficient to order it geographically and present it accordingly, on the assumption that its implications will then be self-evident to any reader who is prepared to examine it with sufficient care.[1]

---

[1] There is much disagreement about this. We should note, however, that analysis and editing seems to be the usual procedure in the production of dialect *descriptions*; there is no obvious reason why they should be proper to the one kind of activity and not to the other. The material itself should of course be carefully preserved in a permanent archive and be accessible to all serious students; it would be most unfortunate if the publication of results, in however monumental a form, should lead anyone to believe that such an archive was no longer necessary, and (as has often happened before in similar situations) that the material in it might as well then be destroyed.

Certain errors in its interpretation are liable to be made by scholars who have not been directly concerned with the collection and ordering of the material; there is a far greater danger of this if it is published without comment than if it is presented with whatever remarks and reservations seem helpful and to the point by those who have been so concerned. It is not suggested that the editing should be in any way similar to that done in producing a large-scale dictionary, but it is felt that it will frequently be necessary to call attention to certain items which for one reason or another are in danger of being misconstrued; there also seem to be good reasons for indicating in a commentary any possible lines of interpretation which have occurred to those who, after all, have given a good deal of attention to the whole matter from the start.

Till recently it has been customary to present the main mass of material on maps. In theory this is a good way of seeing at a glance how distributions work out geographically. In practice, however, there are several objections. The making of such maps is a very expensive undertaking. Furthermore, these tend to be so cluttered with information that there is no question of seeing anything at a glance; this is true even of surveys made by field workers, where the density of coverage has been relatively light; it would be a much more serious problem if one attempted to incorporate the far more copious material amassed by means of a postal questionnaire.

On Ordnance Survey maps there is a system of grids for the British Isles which splits up the country into squares of 100 kilometres, each of which is in turn divided up into 100 squares of 10 kilometres, and so on. It is therefore possible now to give an accurate numerical grid reference to each place from which information has been collected, and these references can serve as a basis for the construction of systematically arranged distribution lists suitable for publication; a key map will of course be provided separately. There may also be good reasons for presenting summaries of the most important information in map form, but the equivalent of each large detailed map used in the older system will be a series of numerical grid-references in columns with the appropriate linguistic entry opposite each reference.[1]

---

[1] The problem of "the manner of presentation of linguistic material collected geographically" is discussed by Professor J. Orr, *Actes du VIème congrès international des linguistes* (Paris, 1949), pp. 545 ff. He points out the defects of the map system and advocates some form of presentation on the lines of that described above.

Chapter 7

CONCLUSION

i

There are certain differences between dialects which I have merely touched upon so far which require some further discussion. Of these, two are of importance, those of a "morphological" and those of a "syntactical" kind. I shall begin by considering morphology, which is concerned with the way words are inflected and the way they are constructed (out of stems, suffixes, prefixes, etc.). These two branches of morphological study are both important in linguistic geography, and in Scottish dialects there are many contrasting phenomena falling within their scope. When we are investigating these, we need as always a fixed point of reference, and in this case it is not dissimilar to that employed in the study of word geography. Let us consider a few examples.

By the inflexion of a word is understood that formal modification it undergoes according to the particular function it has in a given context, so that we may say that different morphological manifestations of "one and the same word" are possible, for example, English "cat—cats," "gaze—gazed," "take—took—taken." Of course it is possible to say that in these three groups of words we are in fact dealing with *seven* distinct words, but there are good reasons for preferring in general the other way of looking at the matter, and regarding, for example, "take—

99

took—taken" as a set of forms of "one and the same word."[1]
It may happen that the difference between different
members of a set involves the presence or absence of a
suffix; "cat—cats." Or it may involve a variation in
the middle of the word; "break—broke." Or it may
involve a much more radical difference in form; "she—
her," "go—went." In certain cases, of course, it is not
easy to decide whether we should regard two or more
"forms" as members of a set in this way, or whether we
should regard them as lexically distinct.

In linguistic geography we are not directly concerned
with sets of forms as such, but rather with the existence
in different places of distinct forms which have nevertheless
the same morphological function. We may note, for
example, that the plural form of *shoe* in Scots is in some
places *shuin*, in others *shoes*, and in ordinary language
we should describe this situation by saying that these
places "have different ways of forming the plural of the
noun *shoe*." These different ways (cf. *coos* and *kie*:"cows")
are our contrasting phenomena, and others are to be
observed, like *threw* and *throwed*, of which we should say,
again in ordinary language, that different places "have
different ways of forming the preterite of the verb *throw*."[2]
In cases like this, we are operating with a fixed point of
reference of a rather complicated kind: first, we assume,
in *shuin* and *shoes* for example, a plural function common

---

[1] The technical term for a group of such forms is *paradigm* or
paradigmatic set.

[2] In many such cases, the geographical distribution of such
forms will not be precise: two or more forms will often co-exist in
the same community, though each may tend to be confined to a
particular "layer" of dialect.

to each form; our fixed point of reference therefore includes the element "plurality." If it happened that every noun in Scots had either a plural in -s or a plural in -n, depending on the place, then we should need no other point of reference; it would be sufficient to compare the plural of any noun in one place with that of any other noun in another place. In fact, this is not so, and for the most part morphological devices must be examined, for the different areas, in operation in particular words. It might be possible, from a morphological point of view, to make something of a comparison of the preterite *threw* in one area with that of the preterite *blowed* in another, but there would be no guarantee that the area using *threw* would also use *blew* or that that using *blowed* would also use *throwed*.

In general, therefore, one must operate in any given case with a particular word (or of course a series of them). The "one and the same word" we choose for an examination of its morphological peculiarities in different places then becomes the other element in our fixed point of reference. We must note of course that by "particular word" we do not imply that it is necessary for even one member of our set of forms of "one and the same word" (for example, the infinitive *to throw*) to be absolutely identical phonetically in each dialect before we can draw any conclusions from the contrasting phenomena elicited by an examination of some other member (e.g. the preterite *threw—throwed*). If we are dealing with contrasting phenomena like *went—gaed*, it may be difficult to decide whether these are of a lexical or a morphological kind[1]

---

[1] Especially if the corresponding infinitives are also different, say *gang* and *gae*.

101

(in a sense they are both). But the distribution of these two forms is likely to be interesting in any case, and will not be in danger of misinterpretation provided the one form is regularly used in one speech-type in all situations where the other form is used in another. In such a case, it will be perceived that we are prepared to fall back on the same kind of fixed point of reference as we used in investigations of Type 2, the basis of which is "one and the same meaning."

Morphologically contrasting phenomena of the kinds illustrated are very numerous and the information provided by a systematic study of them is likely to be important. In particular, it will probably throw light on the co-existence and interplay of different types of speech in a given area. People on the whole are perhaps more conscious of standards of "correctness" in the matter of inflexions than they are in that of vocabulary, and though they may be equally aware of such standards in pronunciation, they find it harder to make phonetic than morphological adjustments to their own speech. Morphological features of the kind discussed therefore tend to show a considerable variety in any one area, and even in one speaker, and an examination of this variety should prove fruitful. Here is a case where a field-worker questionnaire applied in the conventional way (see page 46) is not likely to be wholly adequate, both because of the thinness of sampling and because of a situation unnatural to the informant which even in the most favourable circumstances may prevent him from producing his normal morphological forms. In Chapter 5 we have discussed the possibility of collecting information of this kind by means of a postal questionnaire; in the end, it is probable that such a method, used in conjunction with the efforts of a field worker not unduly cramped by rules of procedure, will be the best practical solution.

The other kind of morphological phenomenon which requires investigation is that which is sometimes called the *derivational* (as distinct from the *inflexional*) type; this involves a study of the formation of complex words irrespective of any grammatical inflexions they may have. An example is the formation of diminutives in Scots, e.g. *lassie, lassag, lassagie* or of compound prepositions like *outwith* or *forby*. The distinction between these and the inflexional type is not absolute, but it is useful. In Scots dialects there are comparatively few phenomena of this kind which would be worth while investigating from the point of view of linguistic geography, and what there are could probably mostly be handled by means of a postal questionnaire. In the case of diminutives, we should note that there are two points of interest not covered by the simple question "by what suffixes are diminutives constructed?" One is "is there in a given area a marked tendency to use diminutives of one kind or another, or is the practice rather to avoid them altogether?" The other is "is there any way of forming diminutives or something equivalent thereto other than by the use of suffixes— as, for example, *wee lass*?"

The possible functional equivalence of *wee lass* and *lassie* calls our attention to the close relationship between syntax and morphology. For what is achieved in the first case by one expedient is achieved in the second by another. It is as well to remember the many intimate functional connexions of this sort, not merely between syntax and morphology, but between both of them and

103

vocabulary. The investigation of syntax itself is one of the hardest of the problems which confront the linguistic geographer, partly because it is often difficult to find adequate fixed points of reference to start from, partly because it is difficult to elicit examples of particular syntactical phenomena by any method, and partly because it is difficult ever to be sure that what is elicited once or twice or even three times is in fact the informant's usual construction. In the field of syntax perhaps more than anywhere else the need is obvious for a series of careful and comprehensive studies of the usage in certain places. If he were provided with these, the linguistic geographer could begin to make a selection of problems which he might then follow up in his own way. Meanwhile he must content himself with a few cases where the above-mentioned difficulties are least severe and hope gradually to assemble more for later investigation.

ii

I have noted from time to time that the evidence of linguistic geography cannot always be interpreted properly unless the investigator is in possession of other kinds of information as well. In this respect no evidence is more directly important than that assembled in a set of adequate dialect descriptions. It is not practicable of course to make an unlimited number of these; what is necessary is a series of them, each made in a different region, so that no considerable expanse of territory is without a description of a dialect spoken in some place located in that territory.

These descriptions should be made on parallel lines, so that the material in each can be compared readily (see page 11); but phenomena peculiar to one area which require special attention must receive it, so that the plan of each description should not be in any way rigid.

We have already seen that most so-called descriptions of dialects have selected for study only a limited number of characteristics and have often treated even these from a somewhat restricted and (in a sense) arbitrary point of view. It is, of course, perfectly true that dialect descriptions, like studies in linguistic geography, must be *selective* in their approach; all I wish to do here is to question whether the actual traditional basis of selection is the proper one, and to discuss whether something better can be achieved. The maker of a description of a living dialect has the advantage of having a very large mass of material at his disposal; he may be forgiven if, faced with all this, he decides that he cannot treat everything adequately.

When this happens, he usually falls back on traditional approaches and on this basis decides what it would be heretical to neglect; he finds, for example, that he is expected to subject the pronunciation of the dialect to a certain type of analysis, but he will probably be comforted to notice that it does not seem to be expected of him that he should investigate certain other phenomena with anything like the same thoroughness. On the phonetic side, he will find that he can ignore many problems altogether, such as intonation, voice-quality and the like (see page 52) without incurring much criticism from his fellow scholars. He is not required to provide the reader with an account of the pronunciation or meaning of anything like all the common words used in the dialect. He will find that an analysis of the syntax of the dialect is rarely given, and if it is, it confines itself to the enumeration of a small number of what are often described as "peculiar constructions," that is, constructions which are not found in less dialectal (i.e. less "broad") forms of Scots.

He will also notice that an attempt is rarely made to give anything like a systematic account of the different "layers" of dialect which may co-exist in one place and which may be noticed by listening to more and to less resistant types, or even to one and the same person on different occasions. It may well be claimed, of course, that the whole business is complicated enough even if attention is confined to the speech of the more resistant types. But it is not possible, for a given place, to decide what may safely be regarded as a resistant type of speech without first making at least a cursory investigation of all the types that are to be heard there. We have also noted that the speech even of a resistant type is liable to vary from one occasion to another, so that the problem cannot be skirted even by singling out some promising old man and ignoring everybody else.

The reasons for the inadequacies of many dialect descriptions are thus fairly clear. First, the whole business is very difficult, and adequate techniques are not available to handle some of the problems. Secondly, even (or perhaps especially) if they were, the work of making a dialect description which (though still not complete) was reasonably comprehensive, would be very great. Thirdly, traditional methods of approach have been inherited and accepted which lag behind not only what is desirable in theory, but what could be achieved in practice. It is not suggested that these methods are by any means wholly invalid, but we may say that they are insufficient in the same sense as the methods of description used by nineteenth-century archaeologists would be regarded as insufficient by an archaeologist of to-day. Here we must make one point which must apply to any branch of linguistic study except perhaps a purely abstract and theoretical one. The consciousness of a lack of adequate techniques must not prevent the investigator from doing his best with whatever means he has at his disposal: he must use the best methods which are available at the time, or which he can devise; he should be prepared to scrutinise and revise these continually, but he must *act*, even though he is conscious that his successors a hundred years hence will criticise what he has done, just as he himself may criticise the work of earlier scholars.

Since comprehensive descriptions of individual dialects are such large undertakings, we must consider what can profitably be attempted on a less ambitious scale. Descriptions which confine themselves to some particular aspect or aspects of the system of a dialect, such as have hitherto been the rule rather than the exception, should continue to be made. This will or should require a good general knowledge of the dialect, but the investigator's attention can be focussed upon it with certain problems specially in mind. It has already been suggested that the favourite forms of approach in making partial descriptions are not the only or necessarily the best forms. A few studies devoted specially to the co-existence of "broad" and "less broad" forms of a dialect in one place would be valuable. It is also necessary that we should have a series of phonetic studies made on a purely descriptive basis, quite without regard to the antecedents of the dialects studied; such studies are already common enough in other countries and are of course obligatory in approaching a living language with no known antecedents. The syntactical system of certain dialects ought to be studied: it would be particularly interesting to do this in some area where Scots is now spoken but where Gaelic or Norse was once in use; in this way new facts might emerge about the influence of the lost language upon the one surviving in that area. Moreover, the abundance of dialect material available for investigation might well be used for specifically experimental studies where the techniques would be very much on trial. For example, there are problems about which the social anthropologist and the descriptive linguist have not yet put their heads together and where they profitably might, as in the case of studies bearing upon the various uses of language other than for the communication of information.

All this implies therefore that current conceptions of what dialect descriptions should contain are open to criticism and that the results provided by such descriptions are correspondingly unsatisfactory. From the standpoint of the linguistic geographer, what is wanted is a series of landmarks from which he can take bearings on any of his voyages of exploration, for in carrying out his studies, he must continually make the fullest use possible of knowledge already available. All his investigations must to some extent lean on such knowledge; to him the existence of such descriptions as are already available is of great importance. But for some aspects of his studies he gets little help from them, and for some areas where he must work there exist no descriptions good or bad. The activities of describing and comparing supplement one another, and a discussion of the nature and aims of distribution studies, to which the bulk of this book has been devoted, only makes the need for further descriptive studies more clear; it is therefore part of the task of a linguistic survey to give some attention to these.

I have already advocated the active pursuit of certain other related linguistic studies. It is a curious fact that one of these not hitherto mentioned, the study of the historical development of the Scots language through the period of nearly six centuries for which considerable evidence about it is available, has received comparatively little attention. For this reason, the elucidation by dialect geography of Scots linguistic problems of a dia-chronic kind is much less easy than it might otherwise be; the history of the language has not been sufficiently studied for us to know what all the problems are. Here then is another good example of the way in which the concurrent pursuit of two quite markedly different lines of research is highly desirable.

Earlier in this chapter I spoke of the question of in-adequate techniques. Scholars interested in the earlier periods of the English language are often heard to lament the inadequacy of the extant information available for the English of Shakespeare's or of Chaucer's time, especially on such matters as pronunciation. For some periods there is scarcely any secondary information at all in the form of grammars or other accounts of the language written by people living at the time. For other periods, that of Shakespeare for example, a good deal of information of this kind is available, but it leaves us in the dark about many things, thus sometimes causing the modern scholar to bewail the shortcomings of his Elizabethan and Jacobean predecessors.

I have already suggested that our own efforts are in turn unlikely to satisfy completely the requirements of our successors, and it is certain that our own shortcomings will be criticised accordingly. But there is one specific measure we can and should take to compensate to some extent for our deficiencies. We are the first generation to be in possession of a technique for making mechanical speech recordings which have a high degree of fidelity. We can therefore hand on to posterity what we ourselves would like to have inherited from earlier centuries—recorded specimens of many different regional and class dialects. No part of the activities of a linguistic survey can be regarded as more basically important than the careful and systematic building up of an archive containing samples of as many different varieties of spoken Scots as possible. For after the scholar of two hundred years hence has quite lost patience with our efforts at analysis, he will be able to turn with relief and edification to the more direct evidence which, on tape, wire or disc, we have managed to salvage for him out of the past.

APPENDIX

At the time of writing, the replies from the first postal questionnaire (see pp. 78–81) are not yet all in, and so far we have done nothing more than make a preliminary analysis of a few items from it. But three maps are presented in the following pages in order to illustrate the kind of information which is accumulating. No attempt is made at any full interpretation of the maps since this can only be done after similar information is available about a large number of different dialect phenomena.

It will be noticed that very little material is presented for the bulk of the Highland area; this is because there are few places in the Highlands where Scots dialect usages are at all common (see Map 2, obs. 2). The vocabulary of "Highland English" differs little from that of Standard English and such peculiarities as there are in pronunciation are not for the most part characteristically Scots at all, but are due rather to the influence of Gaelic. The relevant portions of the maps from the point of view of the distribution of Scottish dialect features are therefore mostly south and east of the Highland Line,[1] and they coincide fairly closely with those areas marked in colour on the dialect map printed in the *Scottish National Dictionary*.[2]

Each map is based on information received from about thirteen hundred informants. I should add that Orkney and Shetland have had to be omitted from the maps purely for reasons of space. The material from Northern Ireland was not yet sufficiently abundant for analysis when the maps were being prepared.

---

[1] The main exceptions are the eastern parts of Ross and Cromarty and of Sutherland. The north-eastern part of Caithness, which lies to the east of the Highland Line, is, of course, markedly Scots in dialect.

[2] VOL. I, opposite p. xxv.

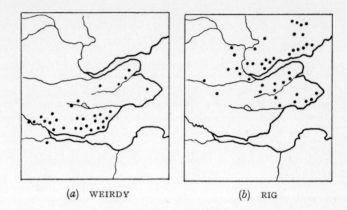

(*a*) WEIRDY   (*b*) RIG

MAP I: OBSERVATIONS

1. The number and variety of different words in living use is not unusually high for a term of this kind.

2. The area in which each word is used is fairly sharply defined, even though certain areas use more than one word: e.g. the overlap of *weirdy* and *rig* in Fife, for which see Figs. (*a*) and (*b*) above.

3. In the area of the South-West left blank on the map no dialect word seems to survive. Part of this territory is uninhabited, see notes to Map 3.

4. The two areas where *rig* is still in use may originally have formed part of a large single *rig*-area which has since been split up by the intrusion of other words from the South-East.

5. At least two of the North-Eastern forms, *eeshan* and *shargar*, are Gaelic in origin; it is probable that *curneed* and *dorneed* are also Gaelic.

112

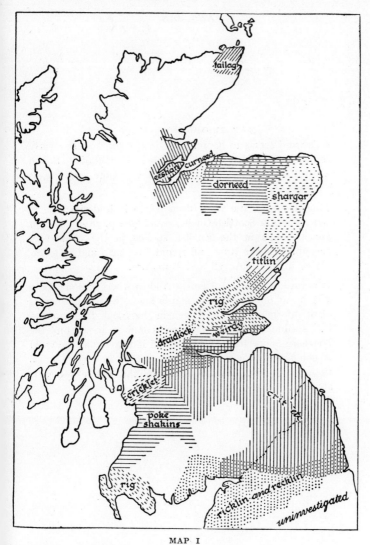

MAP I

Words meaning "youngest or smallest of a brood or litter"

113

MAP 2: OBSERVATIONS

1. This word seems to be unknown in the six most southerly counties. Nor is it used in Caithness or Shetland, though a word of similar form, *arro*, with the same meaning, is common in Orkney.

2. Though *eireag*, the word from which it is derived, is in general use in Scottish Gaelic, *errack* (see p. 78 *n*) does not appear much in the English spoken in the Highlands, except in Easter Ross and round Inverness and in a few places in South Argyll and Buteshire.

3. It is rare in Fife and Angus. And in Aberdeenshire, only fifteen out of seventy informants knew the word, whereas eight informants out of eleven in the Black Isle reported it. Assuming that it was once common in all but the Southern Scots dialects, this would indicate that the word is going out of use much more quickly in certain areas than in others. Its frequency in the Forth valley is striking.

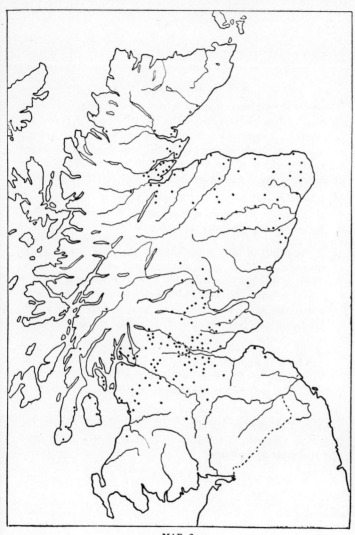

MAP 2
Errack = "pullet"

115

MAP 3: OBSERVATIONS

There are three clearly distinct forms: (1) *wha, whaw,* (2) *whae,* (3) *faa*. Minor variations within the three major types are of course too small in many cases to be noted in a written questionnaire, and it seems best to distinguish only these three main categories until the phonetic details have been thoroughly investigated by a field-worker.

(1) *wha* is closest to the Old English form of the word. In many parts of the area in question the vowel has been raised, giving the form *whaw*.

(2) is the result of the modification of the vowel **ɑ:** discussed on page 59; this form is characteristic of the South-East. There is a broad belt across the centre of Scotland where it co-exists with (1); *twa* and *twae* co-exist in this area in much the same way. A small area in Galloway is left blank on the map because it is mostly uninhabited.

(3) is the North-Eastern form, in which the initial consonant has been changed from *wh* to *f*. It will be noted that the same form is commonly found in the North-Eastern part of Caithness; it is not used, however, in Shetland or Orkney.

The use of (1) along the coastal area of Morayshire and Nairn-shire and in part of the Black Isle is probably due to the linguistic influence of comparatively recent settlements from the midlands of Scotland.

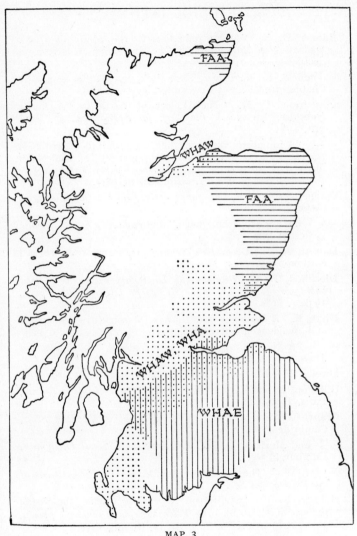

MAP 3
Forms of the word for interrogative "who"

117

BIBLIOGRAPHY

Adams, G. B. "An Introduction to the Study of Ulster Dialects," in *Proceedings of the Royal Irish Academy*, 52, Section C, No. 1, 1948.

Bloomfield, L. *Language*, New York, 1933. (See especially Chapter 19, "Dialect Geography.")

Borgstrøm, C. H. "The Dialect of Barra in the Outer Hebrides," in *Norsk Tidsskrift for Sprogvidenskap*, Bind VIII, 1935.

—— "A Linguistic Survey of the Gaelic Dialects of Scotland: (1) The Dialects of the Outer Hebrides; (2) The Dialects of Skye and Ross-shire," in *Norsk Tidsskrift for Sprogvidenskap*, suppl. Bind I, 1940, and II, 1941.

Craigie, Sir W. A. *Dictionary of the Older Scottish Tongue*, Oxford, 1931.

—— *s.v.* "Scottish Language," in *Chambers's Encyclopaedia*, 1950, VOL. XII, pp. 332–4.

Dauzat, A. *La Géographie linguistique*, Paris, 1922, revised edition, 1944.

Dieckhoff, H. C. *Pronouncing Dictionary of Scottish Gaelic based on the Dialect of the Glengarry District*, Edinburgh, 1932.

Dieth, E. *A Grammar of the Buchan Dialect*, VOL. I (Phonology and Accidence), Cambridge, 1932.

—— "A New Survey of English Dialects," in *Essays and Studies*, VOL. XXXII, 1946.

Dwelly, E. *Illustrated Gaelic Dictionary*, Glasgow, 1901–11.

Gilliéron, J., and Edmont, E. *Atlas linguistique de la France*, Paris, 1900–12.

Grant, W., and Dixon, J. M. *Manual of Modern Scots*, Cambridge, 1921.

—— and Murison, D. D. *The Scottish National Dictionary*, Edinburgh, 1931.

Gregor, W. "The Dialect of Banffshire," in *Transactions of the Philological Society*, London, 1866.

Holmer, N. M. "Studies on Argyllshire Gaelic," in *Skrifta utgivna av k. humanistika Vetenskaps-Samfundet i Uppsala*, 31, 1, 1938–9; *The Gaelic of Arran*, Dublin, 1957.

Jaberg, K., and Jud, J. *Der Sprachatlas als Forschungs-instrument*, Halle, 1928.

Jackson, K. H. *Contributions to the Study of Manx Phonology*, Edinburgh.[1]

Jakobsen, J. *An Etymological Dictionary of the Norn Language in Shetland*, London, 1928–32.

Jamieson, J. *Etymological Dictionary of the Scottish Language*, Edinburgh, 1808. Supplement, 1825. Abridged edition by J. Johnstone, 1846. Johnstone's abridgment revised and enlarged by J. Longmuir, 1867.

Kurath, H. *A Word Geography of the Eastern United States*, University of Michigan Press, 1949.

MacDonald, A. *The Place-names of West Lothian*, Edinburgh, 1941.

Mackenzie, W. Mackay. *The Scottish Burghs*, Edinburgh, 1949.

Marwick, H. *The Orkney Norn*, Oxford, 1929.

Murray, J. A. H. *The Dialect of the Southern Counties of Scotland*, London, 1873.

Orton, H., and Dieth, E. "The New Survey of Dialectal English," in *English Studies To-day*, Oxford, 1951, pp. 63–73.

—— —— *A Questionnaire for a Linguistic Atlas of England* (printed for the Leeds Philosophical and Literary Society Ltd.), Leeds, 1952.

Pop, S. *La dialectologie*, Louvain, 1950.

Skeat, W. W. *English Dialects from the Eighth Century to the Present Day*, Cambridge, 1911.

Sturtevant, E. H. *An Introduction to Linguistic Science*, New Haven, 1947. (Contains, pp. 32 ff., a section on "Dialect Geography.")

Warrack, A. *Chambers's Scots Dialect Dictionary*, London, 1911.

Watson, G. *The Roxburghshire Word-Book*, Cambridge, 1923.

Watson, W. J. *The History of the Celtic Place-names of Scotland*, Edinburgh, 1926.

---

[1] Published as a monograph in this series (1955).

Wettstein, P. *The Phonology of a Berwickshire Dialect.* Printed by Schüler S. A., Bienne, Switzerland, 1942.

Wilson, Sir J. *Lowland Scotch as spoken in the Strathearn District of Perthshire,* Oxford, 1915.

—— *The Dialect of Robert Burns as spoken in Central Ayrshire,* Oxford, 1923.

—— *The Dialects of Central Scotland,* Oxford, 1926.

Woolley, J. S. *Bibliography for Scottish Linguistic Studies.* Published for the University of Edinburgh Linguistic Survey of Scotland by James Thin, Edinburgh, 1954.

Wright, J. *The English Dialect Dictionary,* Oxford, 1898–1905.

—— *The English Dialect Grammar,* Oxford, 1905.

Zai, R. *The Phonology of the Morebattle Dialect* (East Roxburghshire), Lucerne, 1942.

ADDENDA

Catford, J. C. "The Linguistic Survey of Scotland," in *Orbis,* VOL. VI, No. 1, Louvain, 1957; "Vowel Systems of Scots Dialects," in *Transactions of the Philological Society,* London, 1957; "Shetland Dialect" in *The Shetland Folk Book,* VOL. III, Lerwick, 1957.

Hockett, C. F. *A Course in Modern Linguistics,* New York, 1958 (Chap. 56, "Dialect Geography").

Jackson, K. H. "The Situation of the Scottish Gaelic Language and the Work of the Linguistic Survey of Scotland," in *Lochlann,* VOL. I, Oslo, 1958.

Laurenson, A. *The Shetland Dialect,* Lerwick, 1943.

McIntosh, A. "The Study of Scots Dialects in Relation to other Subjects," in *Orbis,* VOL. III, No. 1, Louvain, 1954.

Oftedal, M. "A Linguistic Survey of the Gaelic Dialects of Scotland: (VOL. III) The Gaelic of Leurbost, Isle of Lewis," in *Norsk Tidsskrift for Sprogvidenskap,* Suppl. Bind IV, 1956.

Two articles from *Linguistics Today,* New York, 1954: Bottiglioni, G. "Linguistic Geography: Achievements, Methods and Orientations"; Weinreich, U. "Is a Structural Dialectology Possible?"

INDEX

The following abbreviations are used: G = Gaelic, ON = Old Norse

accent, 29, 91.
Aitken, A. J., 5.
Angles, 20.
Atlas linguistique de la France, 50 *n*, 68.

Barbour, John, 11, 17.
blaw, etc., "blow," 60, 101.
bólstaðr (ON), 22 *n* 1.
-bost(a), 22 *n* 1.
branks, "mumps," 76.
Britons, 20.
buffets, "mumps," 76, 77.

clipshear, "earwig," 43.
comparative approach, 12–16, 18, 36–7, 41.
comparisons, types of, 41–4.
contextual variations in sounds, 57.
contrasting phenomena, 41–4, 72–3, 102.
Craigie, Sir W. A., 5.
craw, "crow," 60.
cricklet, "youngest or smallest of a brood or litter," see Map 1, p. 113.
crit, as *cricklet*.
culture pattern, its influence on language, 27.
Cumberland, 79.
curneed, see Map 1, p. 113.

dat, "that," 61.
Dauzat, A., ix, 50 *n*.
descriptive studies, 10, 12, 14 *n* 1, 16–18, 36–7, 62, 85, 96 *n*, 104–9.
diachronic approach, 13, 14 and *n* 1, 16, 109.
dialect boundaries, 21–2, 37, 40, 82 and *n*; "corrupt" and "pure" dialects, 38, 83; "layers" of dialect, 29–30, 32, 85, 88, 100 *n*, 102, 106; regional dialect, 37–8.
dialect geography, 14 *n* 1.
diatopic approach, 13, 14, 16 and *n*, 70.
Dictionary of the Older Scottish Tongue, 5, 10.
Dieckhoff, H. C., 8.
dis, "this," 61.
distribution studies, 5–7, 9, 14 *n* 1, 44, 70, 72, 81, 85.
divergences, phonetic, 54–5, 58–9, 63.

dorneed, "youngest or smallest of a brood or litter," see Map 1, p. 113.
draidlock, as *dorneed*.
dreich, "tedious," etc., 56.
Dwelly, E., 9.
dyke, 42.

Edmont, E., 68.
eeshan, as *dorneed*.
eireag (G), 78 *n*; see also Map 2, p. 115.
English Dialect Dictionary, 46.
equivalents, 41, 42, 63, 78.
errack, "pullet," 78 *n*; see also Map 2, p. 115.
etymology, 12, 25, 72.

faa, "who?," 55, 58; see also Map 3, p. 117.
fat, "what?," 63.
fat, "stout," 63.
field-worker technique, 46, 47–8, 64, 66–9, 88–92, 95–6.
fixed point of reference, 42, 43, 44, 70 and *n*, 71, 74, 100, 102.
forby, 103.
forkietail, "earwig," 43.

gae, etc., "go," 101 and *n*.
Gaelic, 5 *n* 2, 7, 22, 24, 30, 61 *n*, 79, 85, 108.
gaelick, "earwig," 63, 78.
gellick, "earwig," 43, 63, 78.
Gilliéron, J., 68.
glossaries, local, 8–12, 46.
glottal stop, 53.
gowlack, "earwig," 43, 63, 78
Grant, W., 5.
Gregor, W., 8.
Grimshader, 22 *n* 1.
gullacher, "earwig," 43.

Hamarshader, 22 *n* 1.
hi (order to a horse), "turn left," 70 *n*.
historical approach, 13, 14 and *n* 1, 88, 109.
horny gollach, "earwig," 43.

idiolect, 38.
impressionistic transcriptions, 69, 96.
informants, 47, 89–92.

121